THE IMPRINT

THE IMPRINT

The unintended inheritance that's shaping your life

CRYSTAL OAKMAN

HELPING YOU WORK TOWARDS
A HAPPIER & HEALTHIER LIFE

Published by Crystal Oakman

First Printing, 2024

Library of Congress Control Number: 2024906873

ISBN 979-8-990-47230-3

Printed in the United States of America

To my husband and my daughters. My love for you inspired me to be more me than I had allowed myself to be, and it is from that desire that I am able to finally overcome my own Imprint.

Contents

You are not who you think you are.

There are things buried inside you that whisper. They give you words you speak as your own, and they nudge you, lead you, seduce you into thoughts they want you to have. You have formed decisions from their memories and acted from their grievances. They are ghosts that live within you, peeking out from your eyes. They squat in your skin, clouding and morphing what you think, what you see, what you feel.

You are, quite simply, not *just* you. Rather, you are a haphazard, haunted mosaic of a hundred shards of glass. A physical treasure box of experienced lifetimes. A sea of souls trapped in flesh. The fragmented remains of others past live within you. And if you aren't careful, like a puppeteer to a marionette, they will twitch, and you will move.

James

"I'm turning into my father," James says, wearily.

We're sitting in my office, the morning sun glittering through the windows, threatening to lift the somberness in his mood. I've been having sessions with James, a male in his early thirties, for roughly two months now. Very early on, he told me that his father had died, to very little mourning and even less sadness, when James was just six years old. Understandably, then, James's current sentiment about his similarity to his father is pointedly downcast.

"What do you mean?" I asked, though truth be told, I had predicted this was coming.

James, for all his adept self-reflection, had not. Rather he'd encountered the realization like a punch in the face. There he was, getting ready for our session and brushing his teeth, and the next thing he knew, his father had manifested in the mirror—not so much in a physical reflection, mind you, but rather as an echo of James's life as a whole. The epiphany was extremely unsettling, and not just because James had barely known the man. James had also made a concerted effort not to duplicate the things he *did* know about his father.

It all seems to have started with cologne. A simple matter of scent becoming the capstone to a journey that would culminate in this morning's realization. As James went on to tell me, several months before he ever stepped foot in my office, he had a date. An eagerly anticipated, properly old-school, "pick her up in suit and tie" date at that. James had gone to the store and spent half an hour sniffing various fragrances until he found what would become the first bottle of cologne he ever bought. The date went well, and thus the cologne became a regular part of his daily routine—a sort of aromatic good luck charm.

Now fast-forward to a couple months later. James goes to visit an aunt he hasn't seen since his single days. He closes in to give Auntie a hug and she remarks with surprise, "You smell just like your daddy used to!"

As I mentioned, James's father wasn't very well liked, so it wasn't often that there was reason to bring him up in conversation in a manner that didn't begin with "That son of a bitch . . ." As a result, simply hearing the words "your daddy" was enough to fill James with alarm. But James was equally disturbed to hear that there was *any* similarity between himself and the man he regarded purely as a person with whom James shared roughly half his DNA. James's mind reeled. He spent way too long wondering what even *was* the percentage of cologne manufactured more than fifteen years ago that would still be on the market today? And how, after thirty minutes of browsing and sniffing and perusing countless scents, had he picked the same one his father had worn? Had he smelled the cologne as a baby so that it subconsciously wormed its way into his brain? How could his seemingly random choice hold such a unique paternal connection? After about a week of sleep-disrupting noodling, James did what most of us would do: he chalked that moment up to coincidence and dropped the similarity from thought.

But then more "coincidences" popped up. First was a comment from his uncle that James had begun to style himself—both in clothes and facial hair—the same way his father had at James's age, despite James having seen no pictures of his father from that time. And then there was another uncle's rumination one evening that perhaps James had chosen his college major because his father had once gone to school for the exact same subject. James had thought his father was a lifelong vagrant. He hadn't known his father had tried to attend school, let alone aspired to an actual profession that, shockingly, was the same as James was aspiring to.

And then there was last night and what would be the life-changing argument James had with his mother. James had called his mother after a particularly nasty fight with his girlfriend. He had called looking for support, but as he delved into the details of what had happened, his mother stated that he was taking on the same kind of unhealthy relationship patterns that his father had. When James vehemently opposed the comparison, his mother went on to list all the similarities she had seen between James's relationship and the one she'd had with James's father. They were, to James's shock and horror, an absolute match. And it was after this particular revelation that James found himself coming undone and sitting here with me on this otherwise bright and beautiful morning.

But like I said, I knew it was coming. This isn't the first time I've heard this sort of thing - this often unwanted link to someone else. Similar realizations spring up in sessions pretty regularly, like a seasoned boxer hammering away before my clients even put on their gloves. One day, the vision of who they are just takes this abrupt hit. In hindsight, most people can see where it had been stealthily creeping in—an unwanted behavior here, a turn of a phrase there. But then, often at one single swell, there's a realization that you, the completely free-thinking person with thoughts and actions you're sure are your own, seem to have been sabotaged. Something snaked its way in, turning you sour, sometimes even maladaptive. Something has sunk into your bones, changing your life, creating an existence you didn't want.

Back in my office, James admits to a growing fear that he'll now become even more similar to his father, including dying early, having finally cracked under the same pressures. As he says it, his face drops, and I see the all-too-familiar resignation of someone who has given themselves up to an identity, and a future, they didn't consciously choose.

In many cases, the unwanted identities and futures my clients face reflect the people who raised them. And they're not alone there. The experience is so common that in 2020 Progressive Insurance had a series of commercials that turned it into a joke. "Turning into your parents" feels, for many, like an inescapable path. Of course, not all parents are bad, and the parents that are labeled "bad" rarely are absolute in their suckiness. But even in the best scenarios, where parents are loving and kind and caring, there are parts of the parents that their children swear at some point they won't be like. Yet, sometimes, those parts seep in despite it all. The similarity drips like sweat, emerging without intent, a biological process that happens on its own.

For others, these unwanted identities and futures can't seem to be traced to those who raised them, but there's still a felt sense of something pulling them. There *is* an influence. Something seemingly from nowhere, yet clearly somewhere. Drivers more powerful than their own desires, which push and pull them into action. The influencer may be nameless, but it's definitely still there.

During my years buried in the how and why of human behavior, the awareness that we are not always in control of ourselves has been a constant. The words are different, but they all resonate at the same frequency.

Why am I like this?
I know I shouldn't, but I can't seem to stop.
I spent my whole life trying not to be like her/him, but damn it, I've ended up the exact same.
I have everything I thought I wanted. So why am I still unhappy?

I hear these narratives

all

the

time.

Over the past decade, I have helped people unearth the hidden influences that impact their behavior and lives, to understand and if possible break the seemingly inescapable patterns and outcomes that plague their soul. To do that, I start by fitting together all the parts of the person, slowly forming the identity puzzle of who they are. And I'll admit, at times, it can seem like a vain endeavor. "Influence" is a landscape draped in fog, cryptic lines and odd shapes that even when given focused attention don't often resemble anything nameable. Thus, time, determination, focus, and imagination are all needed in the exploration, because a list of all the forces that move, motivate, and manipulate us could fill an abyss. There is influence *everywhere*—genetics, hormones, neural circuitry, nutrition, parenting, environment, trauma, advertising, and countless other elements, each of which, on their own and without the others, tells only part of a person's story.

For a long time, no matter how much work I did with clients, there seemed to be a piece missing from everyone's picture. There was constantly a glaring hole in the middle of an otherwise finished puzzle - a gap so apparent that its absence could not be overlooked. That hole represented behaviors that didn't appear to have an origin. Patterns that were unexplainable. And then, all at once, like staring at one of those 3-D pictures where the image falls suddenly into focus, an idea emerged. This thought unveiled the missing piece, allowing my clients to finally complete their pictures. And my theory of the Imprint was born.

The Imprint is, quite simply, the lives of others influencing you in ways you don't realize. But the Imprint itself is not simple. It's the memories, experiences, and even grievances from those lives, the lives of your ancestors in fact, pressed like fingerprints onto your psyche. It is the intergenerational transmission of actions and behaviors and thoughts, and it gets all of us, quite frankly, into a rather large mess. With this book, I hope to help you not only make sense of your Imprint but also to rise above it, so that you can not only complete your own identity puzzle, but also live a more satisfying, authentic life.

Within these pages I've included stories from real people,[1] anecdotal data, my ruminations and ponderings, and science. Together, these elements weave a rather remarkable tapestry - one that I believe finally reveals all the pieces of who we really are.

---

[1] Identifying information is changed for privacy, and in some cases, more than one person is represented as a single story. The point of these stories is to show connections and the influences we may be missing, and extreme care has been taken to ensure that I am not giving away anyone's identity. These changes don't materially affect the findings or the spirit of a story.

I

The Haunted

> She herself is a haunted house. She does not possess herself; her ancestors sometimes come and peer out of the windows of her eyes and that is very frightening.
> —ANGELA CARTER, "THE BLOODY CHAMBER"

My mind is not my own—not always. I realized this rather quickly and all at once one day when I, for some reason I can't remember anymore, tried to stop a thought before I had it. Go ahead. Give it a shot. Try to stop a single thought before it comes into your conscious awareness. Yeah, I couldn't either. And it made me realize, quite unabashedly, that thoughts are very independent things, popping up without much planning or intent. Thoughts are there before we think to have them. But that's fairly problematic because, since thoughts tend to lead our emotions and behavior, what we think can hugely dictate who we are.

There is a mantra in my line of work: You can't always believe what you think. Mind magicians and politicians understand this concept *very* well. For instance, sometimes our brains tell us what's comfortable to think rather than what's true. In 1974, researchers Elizabeth Loftus and John Palmer performed an experiment to see how reliable our memory is. Participants watched a videotape of a car driving through the countryside and were then asked to answer some questions about what they had seen. To test the brain's accuracy, some of the questions were deliberately misleading, such as asking participants about the color of the barn in the video when there was, in fact, absolutely no barn. Disturbingly, a rather large number of participants not only answered that the barn was red but also, when challenged on their answer, doubled down on their assertion.

In reality, the participants' brains made it all up. The question prompted the brain to "remember" a color when none existed. Rather than expend the energy of searching through memory of the video in an effort to find the barn, the brain picked the easier option: simply answer the question. Barns are typically red, and thus the memory of the video was quickly edited by the participant's brain to now include a red barn. Unfortunately, this study and others since have proven that humans are often easily persuaded because our minds like to take the easy route.

Our brains are conservationists by nature, conserving energy until we absolutely need it. As such, we are oftentimes more reactionary than proactive in our lives. We think and feel and do without putting in a lot of energy wondering why. Even now, as I sit here trying hard to focus on writing this, my mind is a throng of activity—a midtown traffic route buzzing away with car after car of thought. And most times I blindly acquiesce to those thoughts, getting distracted here or giving in to a feeling there. Thoughts wield a great deal of power, influencing what I'm focusing on and thus impacting my goal of meeting my deadline—and further, my goal of publishing this book, and all the goals spawning from that.

Given this heavy level of sway over my life, shouldn't I be paying more attention to where those thoughts are coming from? Wouldn't it make sense to analyze whether they're really necessary to heed? If we can be deceived to fabricate memories so easily, what else might be there, preying on the brain's flaws? What other things might be compromising our minds, influencing our thoughts and thus our actions?

Perhaps these cars of unintentional thoughts are simply the brain processing all the things it notices that we—the self we think of as the self, anyway—do not. After all, a plethora of stimuli hammers our world but doesn't make it into conscious thought. If we actively processed every single stimuli that happened in our life, we would never get out of bed in the morning. Our brains have to forego giving focused attention to a myriad of sounds and sights and sensations that bombard it in any given moment. What if an unintentional thought about flowers occurred because I actually caught a peripheral glimpse of the roses outside my window twenty minutes ago and never registered it? Maybe the feeling of sadness that sweeps over me as I brush my teeth was triggered by a morose face I saw during the day that I didn't at the time notice I saw.

Maybe.

Shortly after my stop-a-thought experiment, I had a fantastical contemplation. What if, as in the classic horror film *Black Christmas*, some of the cars—these unintentional thoughts that bring on subsequent emotions and actions—are coming from *inside* the house. My house. My brain. What if a thought was actually my mother's whispers? What if a sadness was actually a ripple from my father's mind? Thoughts and feelings that were in existence before I was me, reverberating in me like an echo in an endless cavern.

It may seem a bit far-fetched to you right now, but give me some time. As you're about to discover, we carry information within us that influences us way more than we thought. Information transmitted through time and space to shape our lives. Information about experiences. About memories. About lifetimes. Our itty-bitty cells? They contain an entire galaxy of information. An Imprint from the lives—many, many lives—that we ourselves never lived.

* * *

At sixteen, you still think you can escape from your father. You aren't listening to his voice speaking through your mouth, you don't see how your gestures already mirror his; you don't see him in the way you hold your body, in the way you sign your name. You don't hear his whisper in your blood.

—SALMAN RUSHDIE, *EAST, WEST*

Let me pause for a minute and give a little context about the nature of this book. After all, you're about to embark on quite a journey into the self, and that requires knowing a little more about your guide. To start, it's important to note that all fields of study have two sides that work simultaneously in collaboration with and competition against one another. The first, which I will call the Process side, is the broad stroke. It's the one embracing rules and regulations. It's the side that analyzes data and seeks efficiencies and standards. The flip to Process is what I like to call the Nuance side. This side embraces individuality, accommodating with adaptability and change. It thrives in the subtlety not covered by the rigidity of Process and wields the unique, emotional experiences within each field of practice.

These sides extend to the practitioners within fields as well. Most practitioners of any given subject matter lean to one side or the other. Practitioners who thrive in Process are those memorizing steps and cadence. They focus on how to most efficiently carry out their work and to do so in a uniform way. They are predictable and concise. Yet in being so, they often fail to see Nuance, such as being unable to adapt to work that isn't standard or to adjust the work by "feel" rather than sticking to procedure. In contrast, the practitioners who fully tap into Nuance build meaning and emotion into each step of their work. They look at how something can be tailored to better reflect the needs found in each instance. They are adaptable and distinct. But without accounting for Process, they often lack the skills to perform efficiently or to utilize best practices.

As with all things in life, you can't have one without the other. Both sides are necessary, and their polarization results in both harmony and contrast. For example, the Process-driven builder relies on standards and efficiencies to build the strongest house while the Nuance-driven interior designer develops a look and feel that tells the individualized story of a homeowner. Harmony! But there may be things the interior designer wants to do (can we say "open floor plan"?) that the builder struggles to support. Or a build spec may be required that makes a certain look and feel impossible. Contrast. To see this play out, watch just about any show on Home & Garden Television, which features home building and decorating shows and has become meme inspiring for featuring horridly unrealistic scenarios and seemingly idiotic homeowners.

Furthermore, in some fields, practitioners of one side tend to be treated more favorably than those of the other. Most people want their accountant to be Process-oriented, well versed in finance laws and red tape, knowing every code and standard. But most people also want restaurants centered in Nuance, with meals that excite your senses, crafting food that does more than simply provide sustenance.

In my field, we have researchers (Process) and providers (mostly Nuance). There definitely are practitioners who are wholly rigid and provide service from a textbook rather than taking a personalized approach. Luckily, however, I don't think they're as prolific as those on the Nuance side. Now, with the admission that I'm probably a bit biased, I really feel like the mental health field should be best suited to provide answers to the question of who we are and why we do what we do. And in fairness, much of the science that is done regarding mental health is driven at first by what those of us "on the ground" see in the lives of those we help. Researchers then try to provide a scientific seal of approval, to give merit to the anecdotal evidence about the lived experiences of people we work with in practice. But this attempt often fails because the rigidity of science can't account for the intricacies that make up human life. Science tries to break things down into parts—to analyze a single component existing in a sea of complexity. And that works for things you can isolate in a lab. But for the human condition, it's like trying to understand the many details of a vast forest based on information derived from the stem of a single leaf.

So it's not surprising that in the matter of what makes us who we are, what mental wellness practitioners see as true is rarely replicated in a lab. You simply cannot remove the myriad influences that impact a person—let alone a group large enough to be considered statistically significant in a study—to try to isolate the impact of this or that modality, cue, factor, and so on. And so experiments "fail" and thoughts or practices that don't align with what little science exists are disregarded as fringe. As "out there." Or even as heretical.

So I have to say that, sadly, the field of mental health has been no better at providing a thorough enough answer to who we are than the many other approaches to the question. And without a full picture, how could anyone ever hope to make real change? How could we ever fix what feels broken? Process and Nuance are the black and white, the yin and yang, of every subject matter. But since the two apart can't give us the full picture, we must assume that expertise in the quest for understanding who we are is what happens in the grey.

In *Moonwalking with Einstein* (2011), Joshua Foer helps the reader see "memory champions"—experts in the field of memorization—

through the unexpected world of chicken sexing. The details about this particular profession, which I have to assume is a relatively unknown field, is totally worth checking the book out for. I think I mumbled "No shit!" about forty times through just those three pages. But that aside, Foer explains that the expert chicken sexer (a decently lucrative field if you can hack it, by the way) "perceives the world—at least in the world of chicken privates—in a way that is completely different from you and me" (p. 51).

Expertise straddles sides. It grounds itself in the balance of both technique and intuition, control and flow. It is the craftsmen who can create from the unremarkable trunk of a tree a bookshelf that is both functional and beautiful. The doctor who diagnoses a complex medical problem using both education and the otherwise hidden, subtle cues given by the patient. As Foer eloquently states, "Experts see the world differently. They notice things that nonexperts don't see" (p. 55).

This book and even the Imprint itself comes from that noticing, from that expertise. Who we are is a subject that has captured a bottomless chasm of inputs, yet much of the discussion on the topic leans toward a polarity. We find either a technical dissection of the science, such as what each gene does and how it contributes to this or that behavior, or a purely philosophical discussion on the origins of what it means to be human. But we need something more. We need the Imprint because it lives completely in the middle ground. It is the view that takes *both* Process and Nuance and helps us find what we're looking for.

Furthermore, there is an artistry to life. There are painters and then there are those whose brush strokes move one to tears. There are cooks and then there are chefs, who make your taste buds dance and be sated. And in my field of mental wellness, there are practitioners and then there are guides—those who work to resonate with the wisdom not just in the head but in the soul. To elevate the experience of life to a place of wonder and growth. On the subject of life, artistry transforms the existence we know into one of possibility.

It is in this mode of artistry that I crafted this book. To paint on a verbal canvas a different landscape of what is, so that we can be moved to see our world in a new way. In the matter and manner of life, there are rabbit holes and an abyss of knowledge to explore. What I will focus on within these pages, that of our Imprint, is my artist's view of an aspect of our existence that has hidden itself between Process and Nuance. Hidden itself in the grey.

In 1689, the British philosopher John Locke stated that the human mind is a *tabula rasa*, Latin for "blank slate." Locke felt that humans are born with no innate ideas or knowledge and that we only gain knowledge after we've reflected upon experience. But I can say with confidence that Locke was wrong. Your tabula rasa does not exist. You are born remembering, with the lives of your ancestors imprinted upon you. Within the depths of your being, you have been marked, etched with memories and emotions that you have not experienced. You are tugged by movements you did not make and ingrained with information you did not learn. And these marks shape who you are. Influence you here and now. Those who came before you continue their existence through you.

How this happens? Well, we're about to explore the possibilities. And as we do so, we'll also look at ways we can identify and possibly change, or if need be eradicate, the Imprint's influence. Because in the end we all deserve power over ourselves. We all deserve the option to exorcise the ghosts that have been haunting us from within.

Maggie

It's nine a.m. and Maggie half sits, half stands, a semi-colon of energy who never seems to remain still for long. Her smile, infectious and light, absolutely radiates in the room today, and I find myself smiling in return despite the early hour. And before I hear any groans from you, dear reader, let me say I am *not* a morning person by any stretch of the imagination and so yes, nine a.m. *is* considered early for some of us.

Maggie was adopted at birth. The relationship with her adoptive parents was and is healthy and relatively positive and she has never met her birth parents. As adoption is a trauma wound that starts the minute a child is separated from their birth mother, Maggie's and my work together typically focuses on ensuring she has the tools to process hard feelings as they come up. Today we are discussing feelings that have resulted from a rather unpredictable moment.

A few months ago, Maggie's adoptive father died. This past weekend, while she and her family were going through his storage shed, Maggie found something interesting.

"I found a letter from my birth mother to me when I was just one or two years old," she tells me.

"You didn't know about it?" I inquire, surprised.

"Mom had mentioned a long time ago there was one, but she said it was lost in their divorce. She couldn't remember what was in it, and Dad had said he couldn't find it either."

"What did it say?" I query tentatively. Though a letter from a long-lost parent could provide a great deal of excitement and satisfaction for a child (even an adult one), it also could create a great deal of grief and hurt, depending on what is said.

"Most of it was just about how she loved me and hoped to see me one day." She pauses, drinking in the warmth of that statement. "That was really nice to see, ya know?"

I nod.

"But get this," she says excitedly, her attention snapping back to what she's about to tell me. "She put in lines from musicals throughout the letter. She even wrote out a stanza of a song she was writing!"

For a heartbeat, we sit silent. She is seeing her missing piece. We are, together in that moment, witnessing the impact of her Imprint, and the gravity of that is heavy enough to stop time. Let me explain.

Maggie's adoptive father was integrated into local theater, and she grew up as part of the theater community. She had a propensity for the stage, and by six years old she was acting in local productions and was by her account considered a natural. Theater was a core part of her identity throughout childhood, and she was always seen as a "chip off the old block" of her adoptive father. Now in young adulthood, her love for the craft had only intensified. Several years ago, after seeing a musical her friend had taken her to for her birthday, she had transitioned her attention to that genre, choosing two years ago to work with and in musicals exclusively.

With her birth mother's letter, there was a new factor to consider regarding her seemingly self-chosen path.

"No one writes musical lines in a letter unless that's something you live and breathe," Maggie says, her excitement palpable.

Like you do, I think, seeing the sentiment reflected in her eyes. In that radiant smile.

"I always thought I took to acting because of Dad, but it was there, in me, the whole time," she muses. "Did I do all this because I was raised in the theater? Or would I have done it anyway because it was always there in my genes?"

2

The Undying Debate

Look at Satan. Created as an angel, grows up to be the Great Adversary. Hey, if you're going to go on about genetics, you might as well say the kid will grow up to be an angel. After all, his father was really big in Heaven in the old days. Saying he'll grow up to be a demon just because his dad became one is like saying a mouse with its tail cut off will give birth to tailless mice. No. Upbringing is everything. Take it from me.

–TERRY PRATCHETT AND NEIL GAIMAN, *GOOD OMENS: THE NICE AND ACCURATE PROPHECIES OF AGNES NUTTER, WITCH*

W hen putting together a puzzle, people tend to start in the same place—the edges.[2] Edge pieces frame the picture and thus provide beautiful reference points to figure out where to place the other pieces. In the puzzle of *Who am I?*, most people find that the pieces related to genetics and upbringing—more colloquially known as "nature" and "nurture"—form their edges. The pieces of "nature" are most commonly characterized as the "you" that comes from your genes. It's the coding in your DNA that gives you brown versus blue eyes, or the propensity for a weak heart despite healthy behavior. It's what shows up when you spit in a tube to perform an ancestry test or give your family history at the doctor. The pieces of "nurture," on the other hand, are the "you" that comes from environmental influence. It's the effect of a loving parent versus an absent one, or the difference in eating habits you get whilst growing up during the Depression instead of a time of excess.

Thinking about yourself in the context of nature and nurture is remarkably instinctual, and outside of reading this book, you've probably already done quite a bit of it. You've deferred to nature when claiming to have your mother's gift for carrying a tune or your father's smile. You've referenced nurture when you surmised your own short fuse is the result of the parent who shouted when angry and upset. If you've ever said, "I am . . . because of . . . ," you've embarked on the nature versus nurture discussion. And so it makes sense that people looking to understand themselves begin here, feeling confident that outlining nature's and nurture's influences will be the key to solving their identity puzzle.

---

[2] I once met someone who went into a puzzle all willy-nilly, just picked a piece and started there. I sat there dumbly as if watching a magic trick being performed by a dolphin. It was wild.

But the seemingly clear pools of nature and nurture are, in truth, murky, their waters muddy with the detritus of life's complexity. Pieces that look like they belong together can fool the eye and end up being incorrect, masking subtle distinctions that are mockingly hard to define. Do you like blueberries because your mother liked them and it's in your genes, or is it that, because she liked them, they were always in the kitchen and thus you came to like them too? Did you learn to be a nurturing parent because your caregivers were nurturing, or did the ability to nurture make up your temperament at birth? To delve into what degree of influence nature and nurture have on any one person is to immerse yourself in a chicken-or-egg quagmire. Arguments have been made for each side in turn, a perpetual back-and-forth across humanity's collective net. Determining just how much nature or nurture influence someone has been the subject of a rather scorching debate. One that has spanned millennia.

The phrase that encapsulates the debate—"nature versus nurture" —was popularized in the Victorian era by Francis Galton.[3] Interestingly, Galton was a cousin to Charles Darwin, a man whose name is almost always present when the discussion of human behavior and development come to pass. Now, Galton may have been given notoriety for coming up with such a slick, easy-to-remember name, but he didn't actually come up with the idea. Arguments on whether nature or nurture have the larger influence had been dripping from tongues all over the world well before his time, even before the calendars shifted to mark what historians call the Common Era (a nonreligious alternative to AD).

For instance, one of the many proponents of camp nurture was a man named Chen Sheng, who was born in China around 250 BCE (Before the Common Era). According to the *Records of the Grand*

---

[3] It should be noted that Galton also promoted a racist ideology, but more on that later.

Historian (Watson, 1971), Chen Sheng led a rebellion against the Qin Dynasty in 209 BCE. Dynasties are, by definition, a hereditary faction, with rulers born within the same family rather than chosen from among the general populace. It's an old-school, "our family is better than your family" situation.

Frustrated with what he believed to be repressive leadership, Chen Sheng challenged the people. He asked, "Are kings and nobles given their high status by birth?" This particular sentiment was recorded in *Records of the Grand Historian* because it was clearly an effort to incite rebellion. With his question, Chen Sheng was calling into question a fundamental claim of dynastic rule: that someone is great simply because of who their parents are. His question rejected the notion that greatness was inherent in the Qin family's DNA. Instead, Chen Sheng argued that greatness was available to any man who wanted it, strong and efficient leadership being a trait that was earned by will rather than by blood.

In contrast, another man,[4] born in 428 or 427 BCE, asserted that qualities are not obtained through a lifetime but rather are acquired at birth, and there is quite frankly nothing one can do to change that. This man, Plato—yes, the one and only Greek philosopher and namesake of platonic love—argued that a person is born with a predetermined set of abilities. For instance, being able to learn and adapt (traits required for leadership) are capabilities that you are born either with or without. He asserted in *The Republic* that "the power and capacity of learning exists in the soul already," and that being born with these capabilities makes life easier than for those born without them. And since Plato also believed that the abilities you receive at birth are given to you based on the condition of

---

[4] Sadly, women's writings throughout history—if they were allowed to learn to write—were rarely considered important enough to be kept safe from the destructive forces of time.

your soul, then if you have any difficulty succeeding in life, he felt it is likely because you deserve them.

I could write tomes repeating quotes and stances that argue one side or the other, but I don't have that kind of time, and I trust you get the gist. Suffice it to say, minds likely have been occupied with the nature versus nurture debate since the beginning of human existence. Yet despite the rumination and all the mental power spent by people determined to solve the puzzle, the pendulum continues to swing. It's the philosophical and academic version of the undead. It never, ever seems to die.

Truly unsolvable questions exist, and we humans seem dedicated to finding more. Our species continually pokes holes in the claims people resolutely make on a variety of topics. Resolving a question requires a clear answer, one that is unequivocally agreed upon by everyone. Unsolvable questions don't have this clarity. Take the philosophical question "If a tree falls in the forest, does it make a sound?" Ultimately, the "answer" depends on your understanding of the complexities of "sound" and your views on the nature of being heard. As those understandings differ from person to person, an objectively correct answer remains elusive. There is no singular right answer.

Likewise, on the path to understanding our identity and our behavior, consensus isn't possible. The answer is dependent on a wide variety of variables, definitions, beliefs, and knowledge. It is unique to each person, and thus the question is inherently unsolvable. We can know the factors, such as genes, environment, and now the Imprint, that influence each person, but how much and to what extent each factor influences us is different for each individual, and even varies for each person throughout their lifetime. So I kind of want to smack Francis Galton for coining his term, because there really isn't a debate if no side can win. The simple idea of a nature versus nurture debate is inherently flawed because it supposes that the answer is either/or instead of both/and. And that means this really should be the end to this chapter. But like I said, it's an undead subject.

People don't seem to sit as comfortably with the bothness of this issue as they do with the philosophical quandary of the falling tree. People get nervous when the questions "Who are we?" and "What shapes our behavior?" can't garner consensus. Can't be distilled to a single answer. And so instead of understanding each individual's influences and behaviors in turn, people erect fortresses from generalities and build weapons based on opinions, always at the ready to defend themselves from the opposing side. And so in questions like "How should a youth who comes from an abusive background be held accountable for their own unadaptable behaviors?," the battle becomes a war.

But why do we keep having an argument if we know the answer isn't black-and-white? Why do we struggle to be open to the fact that, in this matter, the truth lies in the grey? This question requires us to take a side quest. And we'll embark on this brief tangent because understanding why the nature versus nurture debate won't die is a key to understanding why much of society has largely overlooked the Imprint.

3

The Shadows

When I had my son I would explain all that to him when he was starry enough to like understand. But then I knew he would not understand or would not want to understand at all and would do all the veshches I had done, yes perhaps even killing some poor starry forella surrounded with mewing kots and koshkas, and I would not be able to really stop him. And nor would he be able to stop his own son, brothers. And so it would itty on to like the end of the world . . .

—ANTHONY BURGESS, *A CLOCKWORK ORANGE*

Here's what I suspect. In the question of why the nature versus nurture "debate" still exists, the main answer is fear. People covet a singular, black-and-white answer because it makes them feel safe. Unlike the philosophical argument over the nature of a sound, in the matter of human behavior, we all have a stake in this game. We care about what makes people act the way they do because we need that answer to help us make sense of ourselves and the world we live in. We need to "know" why people act in the harmful, upsetting ways they do because we think if we can understand the why, we can somehow prevent those harmful, upsetting things from happening to ourselves and our loved ones. We seek to define a black-and-white answer so that we can feel comforted by a concrete, infallible knowing. It's a desire for control within a chaotic, enigmatic existence.

But, you might ask, with all the knowledge that exists today—information so easily accessible in a digital world—shouldn't we have been forced to reconcile this fear by now? We all fear the shadows until we turn the lights on. The shadows of the unknown fail to be monsters when we can see what we're really looking at. And it doesn't take four new moons and a caravan across a desert to get that kind of information anymore. Shouldn't the information be so undeniable that we can finally put this debate that's not really a debate to rest? To slay the monsters in our head and focus on the answers held in the grey? Sadly, no. And I believe there are three reasons why we can't seem to get there, and the first, ironically, is the direct result of humanity's never-ending search for knowledge.

SHADOWS THAT FLICKER

We are a clickbait society; we love a flashy headline. Remember what I said earlier about our brain's propensity to rely on what's easy? Well, our social media and other technology habits have only strengthened that habit. We want to consume information in seconds, not use minutes (let alone hours) of mental energy understanding probabilities and intricacies. Many people won't read far enough into an article to understand the details held within (assuming the article even contains those details). What's more, many people never learned how to properly assess a piece of information, causing them to take at face value the material given to them. And in a society where a catchy headline means getting paid, a lot of the information we consume is written to elicit a false sense of instant understanding. It's written to provide a sense of comprehension in a matter of seconds. And with that kind of timeline, there simply isn't any room for nuance. We just don't have the patience anymore for the grey.

But since so little time is spent on each thing we're consuming, we need a whole hell of a lot of it to fill our days. And luckily for pay-per-click media, with the human condition being ultra complex, there's an endless stream of nature versus nurture content always at the ready, keeping the sense of debate alive.

Take these two studies, published a year apart. The first is a research paper from 2017 titled "Why Nature Prevails over Nurture in the Making of the Elite Athlete" (Georgiades, Klissouras, and Baulch). In its nod to camp nature, the paper states, "Maximal anaerobic capacity and maximal heart rate are heavily dependent on genes, which accounted for 81% and 86% of the variation of traits, respectively," and "the acquisition of motor skills is significantly heritable." Basically, elite athletes are born with bodies that make them able to do their thing. The study, while recognizing that nurture does have some influence on the matter—so those of us *not* born with the ability to have Thor-like heart rate and breathing *might* still be able to be elite in some rare cases—definitively stated, "The overwhelming and accumulating evidence, amounted through experimental research spanning almost two centuries, tips the balance in favour of nature in the 'nature' and 'nurture' debate." Thank you, genes.

A couple of years later, researchers studying the prevalence of myopia (nearsightedness) declared a win for camp nurture with an eye-catching, finale-teasing headline: "Myopia: Is the Nature–Nurture Debate Finally Over?" (Morgan and Rose, 2019). What's fun about this particular discovery was that myopia *used* to be camp nature. Since the 1960s, myopia was thought to be a hereditary condition, and scientists (such as Li and Zhang, 2017) spent their research money and time to look at how genes could cause—or at the very least influence—someone to become nearsighted.

But then, in 2018, researchers Ian Morgan and Kathryn Rose found that cases of myopia in the general public were rising dramatically, and all that they thought they knew went to the crap heap. How could an ailment passed down via genetics suddenly pop up in such increased amounts? If it was hereditary, the number of people with the diagnosis should remain steady with population counts. It was quite the quandary.

What they found was that despite having genetic components, the instances of myopia were rising due to two major environmental factors: school conditions and limited time spent outdoors. The researchers concluded that nurture beat out nature by a landslide, finding that "environmental factors have played a major role in the current epidemic of myopia" *despite* the ailment's heritability.

Now, you astute readers are correct. The papers aren't saying that *all* things are nature or nurture. In fairness, they are speaking only about the nature-versus-nurtureness of their specific variables, elite athletics and myopia. They don't contradict one another. But my point is, in the stories and headlines written for public consumption (and sometimes, as we see, even in the research itself), deterministic statements that might lead someone to a broad-stroke generalization occur frequently. And often enough, headlines are in contradiction, inciting the idea that there's a right or wrong answer.

This conflict is so prevalent that in 2021 the University of Minnesota's Hubbard School of Journalism and Mass Communication hosted a panel entitled "What Happens When Scientific Findings Conflict," noting in the synopsis that "Progress in science is often marked by studies that report similar results and studies that report conflicting results. Yet, media coverage of scientific findings often underscores conflict and controversy—a tendency that is particularly true of issues related to health or the environment." If folks are walking around with, like, four hundred other things that are a priority—which I posit we all are—and don't have the time to dissect and fully comprehend all the variables through which nature and nurture can influence a life, it's very easy to see a few flickering headlines and use those to create a black-or-white conclusion.

SHADOWS THAT LURK

The second contributing factor fueling the eternality of this debate is the one thing we can never get fully rid of: our biases. We are so-o-o *not* impartial when we're faced with questions about motivation of behavior and identity. And we all fall victim to a ton of cognitive biases. For instance, there's a bias called the attribution error, which says we ascribe our own behavior to circumstance (nurture) while crediting someone else's behavior to their nature—something internal to them. When we're not the best version of ourselves, the attribution error leads us to look at all the environmental factors that led up to the situation, all the reasons we behaved the way we did. But when viewing someone else not at their best, we all too often assign them an inherent character flaw. They are, by nature, a bad person.

Let's say you witness a stranger lose their crap in public. The thought most of us would have is that the temper tantrum is due to something being very, very wrong with them. But when *you* have your own Veruca Salt moment, you'll usually focus on *why* you did the thing you did. *Your* emotional outburst occurred because of something that *happened*, not because you're a bad person. "You can't even imagine what I've been through!" you might claim. But that guy from earlier? *That* guy's an asshole.

And angry outbursts aren't the only thing we misjudge other people for. As David Linden surmised in *Unique: The New Science of Human Individuality* (2020), biases make us pretty sucky at understanding on a general level to what degree traits are genetic versus environmental. Linden conducted a survey to figure out where people thought traits came from. He found that the Americans he surveyed were on it enough to figure out that height is strongly determined by heredity, that political beliefs are largely learned, and that musical talent is somewhere in between. But when controversial topics became part of the discussion, the biases fully came out.

Here's a question for you, reader. What's the heritability of body mass index? How much is an individual responsible for their being classified as overweight?[5]

::*Jeopardy* music plays::

Most of Linden's survey respondents answered that heritability of this trait is low, meaning they thought a person's weight is largely influenced by personal choices. Yet the scientific literature indicates that genetics could be responsible for determining more than *half* a person's weight, affecting roughly 65% to 75% of someone's BMI (Schrempft et al., 2018). Linden stated, "Many people want to believe that food consumption is more a matter of personal willpower than it really is" (p. 252). In other words, biases impact what we believe to be fact. And if you, dear reader, find yourself going "Bullshit!" and taking to Google to find a study to prove me wrong, know that this is exactly my point. Our personal biases very much influence our ability to accept, let alone talk about, the grey.

----

[5] I use the word *classified* because I don't have the space or expertise to go into a discussion about the validity (or lack thereof) of BMI as a determinant of health and about what is considered overweight by medical community standards. That's an entirely different rabbit hole.

So it's not just our initial answers that are affected by our biases, it's also our willingness to seek out and accept accurate information. Which is ironic, because we're in the age of information, after all. It isn't hard to find out what research says about the heritability of certain traits. But we don't dig in. We see a flashy headline, maybe two, then formulate our opinion. Then we reinforce ourselves with information that confirms our beliefs. Fortress built.

People overwhelmingly reject information that counters what they want to believe, in part because of two other lurking biases: confirmation bias and cognitive dissonance. The first works exactly as it sounds. We pay attention to information that confirms what we think and disregard information that doesn't. So, for instance, if I believe I'm bad at math but then get an A on a math test, my brain is wired to confirm my original thought. To combat the discrepancy, I'll downplay the A with a narrative about the test being easy or my being lucky this time. A person will rarely take that A as an opportunity to change their beliefs, especially about themselves.

With cognitive dissonance, our brain actively works to defend us from feeling bad about ourselves (as long as that bad feeling isn't part of our personal narrative, such as with the previous example). So let's say I think I'm a decent person, but I've totally judged people for their weight because I have always believed weight was a personal choice. If presented with information that counters my belief—that weight is influenced heavily by genes—I have to reckon with the fact that I may have been a bit of an ass to a person, or to many people, as a result of my beliefs about weight. Thus, in swoops my knight in shining armor, my brain, to defend my honor. It doesn't want me to feel bad about myself because damn it, I *am* a good person and good people don't judge people wrongly—*right?* So what does my wonderful knight do? It slashes away at the information that would make me have to eat humble pie. It's a full-on defensive attack that each of our brains sets up so we don't have to feel bad about ourselves for being wrong. We *all* do it, and it's why facts rarely persuade people to change their opinions.

Fun fact: most readers will find their own brains in this moment trying to find all the times they changed their opinion based on new information, to show that "I'm not like *those* people." Which is funny and totally makes my whole point—and if that was you, don't feel bad. Just recognize it and know you're just like everybody else.

What's more, these biases can have severe, detrimental effects when we don't recognize them for what they are. For instance, when "success" is the trait being scrutinized, the refusal to see anything outside of our beliefs can be oppressive, especially if the people in power use their biases to dictate laws and what programs to fund.

Let's linger on success a moment. Two common beliefs about a person's success—or more importantly, their lack thereof—are that it comes from either pure self-determination or some variation of "God's will." In the first case, you'll often hear people say their success was from "hard work and dedication," with the obvious implication that anyone who hasn't succeeded is lazy and/or undedicated. In this mind-set, typically no recognition is given to any of the other factors that might have helped in that success, despite there being numerous things that can contribute to any one person's success, including luck. Success, in this belief, occurs from pure will-power, innate capabilities, and personal determination. Plato would be proud.

In the other line of reasoning, forces outside of someone's control impact success. In this mind-set, a person has prayed enough, manifested enough, or otherwise done something pleasing enough to their chosen force to garner prosperity. Conversely, the implication (and sometimes the outright explicit statement) is that failure is a result of an unhappy deity, a "test" of your faith, or some other reason you deserve not to succeed. Success, in this belief system, occurs due to otherworldly "favor" and is a mark of being worthy.

These two belief concepts are mutually exclusive, yet ironically, they're often part of the same person's narrative of success and failure. Biases and attribution error at work again. If success occurs for me, it's because I worked hard and/or I am inherently "good." If it doesn't, it's the plan of some otherworldly thing and not a flaw in myself. But if someone else isn't succeeding, it's probably because they're lazy, flawed, or otherwise unworthy of success. If *I* fall on hard times, it's the result of a greedy corporation, a tyrannical boss, the government, and so on. But if someone I don't know falls on hard times, especially if that person comes from a group I have an internal bias toward, it's clearly a fault of their own.

It's an exhausting whiplash.

And there's more. We have yet another bias (a logical fallacy, actually), tokenism, that people often use to further confirm beliefs about nature and nurture's impact on success. Tokenism is when single cases are used to represent the whole, and they're often used to "disprove" a narrative. An example would be "Joe was obese and easily became thin, therefore, *all* people who are obese are able to become thin." Or "Jill made it out of poverty and went on to have a successful career, therefore, *all* people who are in poverty should be able to get out and have a successful career."

With tokenism, we can turn a matter into black and white by focusing on outliers within a subject matter that confirm our already held beliefs. "Jason grew up poor and now he's wealthy, so that means anyone who grew up poor can be wealthy," effectively dismisses all the reasons the path from poverty to wealth isn't exactly overflowing with people. With tokenism, people can judge others more easily because there's an example to "prove" that their belief is correct. It allows us to say that if someone had a specific outcome—a minority getting an executive-level position, for instance—anyone who doesn't get that same result is flawed. It's a direct result of that person's lacking nature.

And as I said, these biases can have detrimental effects. For one, it erases any need to help fix systemic issues. If one person can do it, everyone can, so there is no systemic problem. Further, these biases allow us to avoid empathy and connection. If I believe success is purely a matter of X and Y, I don't have to care about someone who hasn't had success. Their failure is their problem, because the formula is black-and-white. With biases, we get to avoid having to feel any sense of responsibility for the difficult challenges faced by others.

Take for instance the continual pushback against social programs meant to help low-income families. The poor are often labeled as lazy, with poverty characterized as a result of some flaw within the person that prevents success. This view ignores the data that plainly shows that poverty is actually the result of a multitude of circumstances, the majority of which are environmental and external (Heard-Garris et al., 2021; Upadhyaya et al., 2021).

Mind you, the view that poor people are lazy is what I like to call the "until it happens to you" bias. I have known more than a few people who have met a rather sudden and detrimental financial downturn, which is not surprising, given that roughly 61% of individuals in America are living paycheck to paycheck (Dickler, 2022). And those same people who used to lambast poverty programs as being "handouts for the lazy" sing a completely different tune for those same programs once they are the recipients. When it happens to *me*, it's different.

All. Over. Again.

SHADOWS THAT DAMN

With our short attention spans helping us build opinion fortresses, and our biases influencing our ability to have compassion, we get into some pretty scary territory. Because picking a winner in the nature versus nurture debate gives that side the power to judge and condemn. Let's stick with the concept of success.

Pick someone you think has done really well in life. What would you say to yourself about that person if you knew they were genetically prone to success, that something in their DNA gave them the skills to be successful? Now what if, instead, it was not their DNA at all but rather their environment that was the sole factor in their ability to accomplish their goals? What if certain things were put in place for them—things anyone else could have but don't—and those were the factors that gave that person their success? If there was truly only one winner to the why—if someone was either born to be successful or someone had to have the right circumstances set out for them to be successful—that would change a *lot* about how we see others. And you'd like to think that we, as a good, loving species, wouldn't condemn people with that information. But, sadly, history shows us we absolutely would.

From the 1940s until about the 1970s, it was a widely accepted fact in American psychiatry that bad nurturing, vis-à-vis bad mothers, caused schizophrenia (Harrington, 2016). In 1957, John Rosen used the F-scale (F for *fascism*) to study the personality traits of the mothers of male patients with schizophrenia (Dworin and Wyant). Rosen felt that there was no way babies could naturally be born with such a troubling ailment, that there had to be some external cause, and he hypothesized that a mother's inability to adequately love her child was the culprit. As such, he tested whether the mothers of his patients had F-scale scores that aligned with a fascist personality.

His results showed the mothers of his patients did, in fact, score more fascist than mothers in the control group (those whose sons did not have schizophrenia). For Rosen, this was the damning evidence needed to prove that bad mothers were to blame. And this ability to name a singular cause for this particular mental illness was the medicine needed to quell the fears of the general public—a public that I suspect was all too eager to feel safe in knowing they couldn't possibly have a child with schizophrenia. They would not be fascist mothers who hated their children. Problem solved.

Rosen's findings kicked off a "mother blame" that lasted almost three decades. Mothers of children with schizophrenia were labeled "rejecting, rigid, domineering, and anxious, and sometimes all of the above" (Harrington, 2016), and not just by the general public but also by the doctors who were supposed to be helping them. Worse, it allowed society as a whole to not have to care about the people who suffered as a part of the diagnosis. Families that contained a person with schizophrenia suffered emotionally, financially, and mentally, with little external support. *Bad mothers don't deserve support, you see. They get what they deserve*, the public seemed to say. *Why should society give them any help at all?*

There's a scene in the television show *Game of Thrones* where Queen Cersei is punished for adultery by having to walk through the streets, naked and bleeding, while a woman behind her rings a bell and shouts, "Shame!" During her long walk, all the townspeople come out to yell, spit at her, and hurl insults. This is kind of what it was like to be a mother of a child diagnosed with schizophrenia from 1957 to the mid-1980s. As Harrington (2016) points out, it wasn't until Seymour Kety's adoption studies in the 1970s that there was any hope of turning the tide of damnation. His studies, thankfully, countered Rosen's findings and showed a hereditary basis for schizophrenia. Kety found that children born to a mother with schizophrenia but raised in an adoptive home were as equally likely to be diagnosed with schizophrenia as siblings raised by the biological mother, meaning the children were born with a propensity toward the disorder.

Subsequent studies supported Kety's findings, and in 1984, more than twenty-five years after the emotional assault on mothers with children diagnosed with schizophrenia had begun, the shift to a hereditary basis for the disorder was fully accepted. An American television program called *Madness* did a multipart documentary on the diagnosis. In it, clinicians finally publicly apologized on behalf of their profession for having cited bad parenting as the cause. There was, in the end, not a "shred of evidence" supporting the bad parenting hypothesis. The higher scores of the mothers in Rosen's study had nothing to do with lack of love and more likely a condition of being a parent of a child with a severe psychological diagnosis. And though the science eventually righted its own wrong, it couldn't undo the decades of false belief that resulted in the harassment and vilification of parents, especially mothers, of people with schizophrenia. Eve Oliphant, mother of a child with schizophrenia during those embattled years, noted, "We failed to understand why parents of a child with leukemia were treated with sympathy and understanding, while parents of a child with schizophrenia were treated with scorn and condemnation" (Harrington, 2016). As an aside, according to the World Health Organization (2022), even to this day, whether as a sustained result of Rosen's bad science or society's biases against helping people we don't believe can be helped, schizophrenia is one of the least supported areas of community mental health.

So the pendulum swung. Nurture to nature. But as I've alluded, black-and-white answers to questions of human nature are problematic. As evidence, note that the new assumption of a heavily hereditary base for this illness didn't mean that blame and guilt vanished for the parents of someone diagnosed with schizophrenia. It still presumes a singular cause, and so the heritability of schizophrenia brought with it its own blame. Parents grappled with the guilt that a genetic issue ran through their DNA. They were, and frankly still are, seen by many as having an inherent flaw. I'll often hear people remark, "I don't need to pass on any of this mess," and then choose not to become a parent as a result of someone in their family having an undesirable diagnosis. As if something within them is irrevocably flawed and the world doesn't need any more of it.

What a sad thing, to feel like there's something in your core makeup that is so awful that your eternal lack of existence would be a gift to the world. And when we start going down the path of perceived flaws in the core makeup of a human being, things start to get very, very scary.

Galton, the aforementioned coiner of the "nature versus nurture" phrase, used these types of heritability findings to argue for eugenics, or the study of how to increase the occurrence of "desirable" characteristics in the population. And let me tell you what, if the definition raises your eyebrows, know the practice of it is way worse. When folks start taking up a eugenics stance, it usually ends up with an attempt to have groups of people sterilized, segregated, or dead, all to "better the world."

It usually starts innocuously enough. Scientists work to, say, find a genetic marker for polio—which they actually did, back in the 1950s (Cossart, 1967). Everyone could agree that polio is awful, so research to uncover a cause was wholeheartedly supported. And let's imagine that they found a genetic marker. Perhaps science could have used that information to help people avoid having offspring who would contract polio—maybe even find a way to stop that gene from being passed on altogether. Thus, someone might be able to say that a preferred hereditary makeup for any given person would be one that does *not* have a genetic marker for such an awful disease. But whenever someone starts marking traits as preferable or not, you inevitably end up with a list of undesirable traits—and thus undesirable people. What do you do with people who could pass on such a condition, especially a condition that is such a strain on the system? What does society do with people who have a genetic composition that contains something that is deemed detrimental to our success as a species?

We certainly have enough history to tell us where that ends up. There were, of course, the Nazis, who attempted to "cleanse" the world of those they deemed "unworthy," euthanizing at least 70,000 adults and 5,200 children, and sterilizing roughly 400,000 victims (NIH, 2022). But don't be fooled into believing that was a one-off case. The Nazis weren't the only eugenicists in world history. For instance, throughout US history, eugenicists (both secretly and publicly) have been nearly frantic about the increasing birthrate disparities between immigrants and non-Nordic races compared to whites. And by the 1970s, using targeted and misleading science, eugenicists from a variety of disciplines were using diagnoses like "unfit," "feebleminded,"[6] and "antisocial" to involuntary sterilize at least 60,000 people across thirty states (DenHoed, 2016). Hell, it was only in the 1960s that states began repealing sterilization laws. But the repeals didn't outright end the effort to rid the world of people whom some deemed unwanted. For instance, did you know that more than one hundred female prisoners in California were sterilized without their permission between 2006 and 2010 (Howle and Cordiner, 2014)?

The use of the nature versus nurture debate to condemn certain people within society as "less than"? Well, it's a damn big problem. But the desire by society and well-meaning scientists to actively avoid sparking a Rosenesque condemnation results in missing some of the information we could get from a deep dive into each side. When we avoid digging deeply into either side because of the fear that really bad people will weaponize the findings, we can miss seeing some really interesting things. Maybe a lot of things. It keeps us from finding the grey.

----

[6] Feeblemindedness was a "condition" (mostly of the poor, and especially of poor women) that was diagnosed using crap IQ tests and "symptoms" such as moral degeneracy, a desire for sex, or any general discontent or disagreement with someone deemed more important, wealthy, or above one's status.

So let us commit to not shying away. Let us, here together, do our own deep dive. Let us journey together and peer into the grey. Peer into the place where we can finally see our Imprint. Let's start, my friends, with the story of the Jims.

The Jims

In 1940, two identical twin boys were born and, sadly, immediately separated from each other and adopted (Littlechild, 2018). The first was named James Lewis by his adoptive parents and called Jim. Jim grew up in Lima, Ohio, and had a dog he named Toy. As a child, Jim enjoyed math and carpentry but did not like spelling. As an adult, he took a job as a security guard, drove a light blue Chevrolet, and was a heavy smoker. This first Jim eventually married a woman named Linda, whom he later divorced, and then went on to marry another woman, this one named Betty. Jim and Betty then had a son, whom they named James Alan Lewis.

The second twin, adopted by the Springers, also was named James by his adoptive parents. He was also called Jim. This second Jim grew up in Piqua, Ohio, and also had a dog he named Toy. When the second Jim was in school, he enjoyed math and carpentry but not spelling. As an adult, he worked as a deputy sheriff, drove a light blue Chevrolet, and was a heavy smoker. Second Jim went on to marry a woman named Linda, whom he later divorced, after which he married a woman named—you guessed it—Betty. And for the cherry on this sundae, the second Jim and his Betty had a son they named James Allan Springer.

At age thirty-nine, the brothers were reunited for the first time, and after talking, they discovered many other similarities. They both suffered from a very specific type of headache, mysteriously gained ten pounds just before adulthood, and tended to bite their fingernails down to the quick. They both used the same romantic gesture of scattering love letters around the house for their wives and smoked the same brand of cigarettes. What's more, they each spent their yearly vacations in the same place in Florida—astonishingly, within just three blocks of each other (Chen, 1979).

4

Echoes in the Blood

One need not be a Chamber—to be Haunted—
One need not be a House—
The Brain has Corridors—surpassing
Material Place—

—EMILY DICKINSON,
"ONE NEED NOT BE A CHAMBER—TO BE HAUNTED"

Many of us have known twins and have seen them do that cool mind meld thing where they finish each other's sentences and mirror behaviors. But do you ever wonder what makes those similarities occur? Most people would assume it's a mix of both the identical genes and growing up in the same environment. But with the Jim brothers, how were there so many similarities if they didn't grow up together? Could genes really be responsible for making people scatter love letters around the house and marry not one but two women with the exact same name? Perhaps the Jims are a fluke, one of those crazy coincidences where all the things just line up perfectly. But you should know me well enough by now to know that's not the case.

Oskar and Jack are identical twins who were born in Trinidad (Chen, 1979). When their parents separated six months after they were born, there was a true *Parent Trap* situation. Oskar's mom took him to Germany so she could be close to her own mother and get assistance in raising him as a single parent. Oskar's mother and grandmother were heavily Catholic, and he was involved with the church throughout his life. He also became involved in the Hitler Youth movement. Back in Trinidad, Jack remained with his dad. Jack's father never remarried, and Jack was raised Jewish. Jack eventually emigrated to Israel, where he served in the Israeli navy. Thus, unlike the Jims who grew up in similar homes in Ohio, these two brothers were raised a literal and figurate ocean away from each other.

When the two brothers finally met, in 1954, twenty-one years after their separation, you might be surprised to hear there were quite a few similarities between them. Similarities that feel like they would make a lot more sense had they grown up in the same house. For instance, the first time they met, Jack and Oskar unknowingly wore the same outfit (Grimes, 2015). Both men also tended to fall asleep after eating, and they both read the endings of books first. They each enjoyed spicy foods (despite the culinary differences of their childhood homes) and flushed the toilet twice, both before and after use. In addition, the brothers liked to wear rubber bands on their wrists and enjoyed pranks, particularly sneaking up on people and scaring them by loudly sneezing. Despite growing up in completely different households, Oskar and Jack shared not just identical looks but also a large swath of idiosyncrasies—things we think of as individual or learned behavior, not something genetic.

Twins, especially those raised apart, are research gold for scientists trying to find answers in the nature versus nurture debate. Identical twins share almost 100% of their genes, while fraternal twins share just about half, akin to non-twin siblings. In twin studies, scientists look at similarities between identical twins and compare them against both the general population and fraternal twins.[7] Since identical twins share so many genes, similarities that appear even when they're raised apart are suspected to be from genetic causes—it's considered unlikely they would have picked up identical behaviors within disparate environments. After all, how many identical behaviors do you share with random people? Plus, any traits that identical twins share more often than fraternal twins, especially unusual ones like skipping the first page when reading a book, tip off researchers that genetics might be at play. Again, how many identical behaviors do you share with your siblings? If you share the behavior, it's likely environmental. Make sense?

In 1979, Thomas J. Bouchard and his colleagues in Minnesota studied one hundred twins separated at birth and raised apart. Bouchard found that identical twins had the same chance of being similar in terms of personality, interests, and attitudes, regardless of where and with whom they grew up. Then, presumably as a result of some very interesting conversation with Bouchard over drinks at a local pub, researchers from the University of Minnesota kicked off their own and aptly named Minnesota Twin Study in 1989. All twins born in Minnesota at the time were invited to participate, and five hundred additional eleven-year-old twins were added in 2000. In a nutshell, the sample size in these studies was pretty damn big. The studies found a string of traits and behaviors that the researchers concluded are due to genes, not environment (though not everyone agrees with all of these claims). Nature, it seems, has quite a story about how it impacts our lives. But nurture, not to be outdone,

---

[7] Fraternal twins are their own group because although they only share roughly half of their genes, they still have other similar environmental factors that non-twin siblings wouldn't have, such as womb environment and chronological age.

has its own tale to tell.

Mark and Scott Kelly are identical twins who made the news in 2019 after Scott, a US astronaut, finished a record 340 days on the International Space Station. The stay was part of an experiment to better understand physiological processes in space (Hayasaki, 2018). Though Scott's time in space was an achievement, we're discussing him here because of what happened after he was back on earth. I have to imagine that identical twins are wickedly useful to NASA research. After all, there can't be that big a pool to pick from. How many twins have the ability or even the desire to be in a NASA program? In this case, having an astronaut twin gave NASA an opportunity to see the effects of space travel on the body, because they could see what differences popped up in Scott compared to Mark. Both Mark's and Scott's DNA were tested pre- and postflight and then compared again once Scott was back on earth. What the researchers found was astounding. Scott's DNA, the recipe of how to make, well, *him*, had been altered by space travel.

When Scott returned to earth, NASA discovered that the flight had not only created abnormalities in some of his chromosomes—the copy of DNA that each cell has inside it—but also had made a few changes in his genetic core. Marina Koren wrote in *The Atlantic*, "Some of Scott's genes changed their expression while he was in space, and 7% of those genes didn't return to their preflight states months after he came back." So what does that mean exactly?

First, a quick science lesson. Let's say you are not a human but instead are a giant multi-tiered cake (red velvet all the way). DNA is the entire working recipe of how to make your cake (in other words, you), including everything from prep to decorations to how best to serve you (warm, with a cup of tea, please). Genes, the information about certain traits, characteristics, or cell functions that gets passed down from your birth parents, are small segments of that recipe—such as how to, say, make the filling needed for the first tier. Our cells are like workers in the bakery. They all have different jobs and work on different parts of the cake, and they have a printout—called a chromosome—that tells them what their job is that day. The chromosome printout contains parts of the full recipe, including groups of genes. So one of your cells might be told it's on chocolate duty, with the recipe to make the filling for the first tier, *and* also the recipe to make the cake for one of the tiers, and maybe even a few decorations.

Depending on a multitude of factors, the genes that come from your parents—the smaller segments of the recipe—are either in an "expressed" state (turned on and doing what they're coded to do) or are "unexpressed" (turned off). Or, sticking with our metaphor, they are either on the recipe card or are scratched out as not needed at this time. What's more, a gene's expression can change. Some genes are off and then something happens to turn them on, while others are expressed and then something occurs to turn them off.

The study of this expressed or unexpressed state of genes is called epigenetics, a field that includes looking at what alters gene activity (turning them on or off) as well as what communicates that change to cells. The prefix *epi-* comes from the Greek language reference for "on top of" or "above," so epigenetics is simply the process that occurs "on top of" the gene. So, with regard to genes and epigenetics, DNA is the recipe, genes are smaller parts of that recipe (such as how to make the icing), and epigenetics is the pastry chef responsible for each of those parts, for deciding which ingredients on the recipe card are going to go into the icing *this* time. Sometimes even using more of a specific ingredient than the recipe calls for, sometimes less.

Another analogy I've heard to describe the role of epigenetics is that of a symphony, where DNA is the sheet music, genes are the instruments, and epigenetics is the musicians. Instruments need the musicians to play them. What's more, the musicians might play their instruments loudly or softly. There are many things that can influence how those musicians play our genes or how the chef builds our cake today. Exercise, sleep, trauma, environment, aging, disease, and diet—they're all parts of our environment that influence our musicians, our pastry chefs, which in turn impacts what and how each gene shows up in us every day.

So, back to space turning people into aliens. Not really—but man, wouldn't it be something if *that's* where I was going?! Anyway, as *The Atlantic* article mentioned, once Scott returned to earth, just over 90% of his modified gene expressions returned to baseline. However, 7% of Scott's genetic signature didn't (measured six months after his return, by the way), and that 7% encompassed more than eight hundred genes, including some related to the immune system and others whose job it is to repair DNA (Zuckerman, 2019).

What I found a bit unsettling was one of the other things that didn't return to baseline: some of Scott's telomeres, the little protective caps that sit at the ends of chromosomes. They shorten as we age, shrinking the teensy-tiniest bit every time our DNA has to replicate itself in a new cell in order to replace damaged cells, which ends up being roughly two trillion to three trillion times a day (Garrett-Bakelman et al., 2019; King Abdullah University, 2018). Because the radiation, microgravity, and isolation of space all damage cells and therefore Scott's body had to do a lot more of that DNA replication to replace those damaged cells, NASA expected Scott's telomeres to shorten more during his time in space than would have been the case if he'd stayed on earth. However, Scott's telomeres actually grew *longer* in space.

The unexpected elongation eventually reversed after Scott's landing, but instead of going back to normal, some of Scott's telomeres became even shorter than what NASA's calculations projected. Like a funhouse mirror, parts of Scott's body grew younger while in space, but back on earth the outcome reversed entirely and time was taken from him. Shortened telomeres have been associated with all the things we see as we age—declining fertility, dementia risk, cardiovascular disease, and even an increase in some cancers. As of now, NASA doesn't really know (or at the least, hasn't reported) what those changes will mean for Scott in the long term.

So OK. Space—the environment (nurture) that Scott was in—did some pretty heavy messing around with who Scott is and what his future might hold. And physically, he came back a somewhat genetically different (and older) person than he was when he went up. But that's because it's *space*, right? I mean, we can expect things to get wonky once we move into the last frontier. Yet research shows the environment here on earth can lead to changes in gene expression (and thus, your life and who you think you are), and some of these changes are occurring as early as birth.

The Colombia Twins

Picture this. Colombia. 1988.

An expecting mother from a rural village makes the trek to a hospital nearby to give birth. She gives birth to twin sons, but one of the twins immediately becomes ill. The hospital is small and isn't equipped to deal with the illness, so the boy is swooped up by a relative and driven to a hospital in the capital city of Bogotá, six hours away, where, interestingly enough, another mother had just given birth to her own set of twin boys. Now, it's unclear how, but according to Fordham News (2018), the sick twin from the rural village accidently got switched with one of the city-born twins. Thus, when the mother from the rural village goes to the city to bring her child home, she instead unknowingly takes home the city-born twin. The sick twin recovered and was taken home, again unknowingly, by the city mother. Both families, assuming that their twins were fraternal, left the hospital with two nonidentical boys, one boy from each pair of identical twins.

Before I go on, if you are like *No way that would happen*, let me just give you some context. Hospitals back then were not birthing centers with suites where parents could stay with their baby for a day or two after birth, the complete family unit holed up in a virtual Airbnb. Instead, you gave birth in a hospital bed, most often in a room with another person who might or might not be also in delivery. (I still remember when providing a "semiprivate" room for delivery was a new concept offered only by the best of the best hospitals.) Thus, it was completely common for a child to be immediately taken from its mother and placed in a nursery, where all the children born at the hospital were placed. People, including the parents, would be given the opportunity to look at their newly born child through a window, where it was held up for collective gaze by a nurse. It was kinda like viewing a baby panda at the zoo. I tell you this so you realize it's not an absurdity that these two mothers didn't notice that one of their kids didn't look like one they delivered.

So back to the boys. We now have a scenario where each set of unrelated brothers is in an environment that is completely different from the other. Jorge, one of the city-born twins, and Carlos, the sick twin from the village, were raised by a single mother in a working-class neighborhood in the bustling city of Bogotá. The boys attended public school and eventually went on to college, where Jorge studied mechanical engineering and Carlos studied finance. The other boys, Wilber (whose birth mother was from the rural town) and William (whose birth mother was from the city), lived 150 miles away from their identical twins in a remote village on a farm with no running water or electricity. They walked an hour to attend school until they reached fifth grade, after which they left school altogether to work full time on the farm.

Fast-forward to when, after a stint in the military, both Wilber and William decide to leave the rural world behind and work at a butcher shop. And where would that butcher shop be? In the bustling capital city of Bogotá, of course. The place where this whole ordeal started. And it was there, in the summer of 2013, that the two sets of brothers found out the truth behind their identities. Here's how it goes.

A coworker of Jorge goes to the butcher shop where Wilber and William work. The coworker sees William and immediately thinks it's Jorge. William explains that he is not this Jorge person, but the resemblance is just too uncanny and the coworker asks to take a picture of William to show his friend, Jorge. When Jorge is then shown a picture of William, the truth begins to unravel. The two men meet up and are just floored—taken aback by how alike they look. They get along remarkably well, and it could have just stopped there and been one of those crazy "I found my doppelgänger!" situations. But the conversation eventually moved to families, and when the two men saw photos of each other's "twin," that's when it all fell into place.

Given what we've already discussed, you might suspect that the Colombian identical twins shared traits in common beyond looking alike, despite their disparate backgrounds. And that was in fact the case. Despite their socioeconomic upbringing, identical twins Wilber and Carlos were both very interested in their outward appearance. Both of them got their eyebrows waxed and had an interest in fashion. They both were reserved, liked similar types of women, and called themselves "crybabies" because they were emotionally sensitive as children. Wilber and Carlos, whose birth mother was in the rural village, had a long list of various types of ailments and issues within their medical history, and both reported themselves to be quiet but quick-tempered.

Conversely, twins Jorge and William had no medical complaints whatsoever. They were both outgoing, talkative, and less formal overall than their nonidentical brothers. They also both liked to joke around and felt they saw and understood the world in a similar way.

But despite the similarities, there was an undeniable discrepancy among the brothers in this story. Researchers found a difference in the genetic makeup of one set of what should have been identical twin brothers (Segal et al., 2017). One pair of identical twins was epigenetically similar, despite being raised apart in such different places. But in the other pair, the epigenome of the brother raised in the city seemed to differ *significantly* from that of his identical twin raised in the country. And that matters, because epigenetic variations can lead to extreme changes in a person's health, personality, and even appearance. Epigenetic changes can result in things like the development of an autoimmune disease, change someone's resistance to cancer, make someone more prone to neurodivergency, or as in the case of astronaut Scott Kelly, even impact how long you're expected to live.

Epigenetic changes can occur for a variety of reasons. Genes can be affected by all kinds of environmental things, such as ultraviolet rays, pollution, or pesticides. But in the case of the Colombian brothers, if the cause of the epigenetic changes was strictly environmental, why wouldn't the epigenetics of the other set of brothers vary? If something caused one brother's genes to act differently, shouldn't that same thing have caused the other brother, raised in that same environment, to also have a shift? One of the possibilities that scientists are looking at is that the epigenetic changes were actually triggered before the twins were separated, either in the first moments of life or in the uterine environment, such as during a placenta distribution.

In a 2019 interview on NPR's *Hidden Brain*, Nancy Segal, the director of the Twin Studies Center at California State University, talked about a pair of identical twins who had a vast variance in height. One of the twins had an issue in her placenta, which made her undernourished during her time in utero. So by young adulthood, her twin was seven inches taller than her. As Segal noted, the intrauterine environment "was something that had a lasting imprint on these still identical genes." So perhaps if one Colombian brother had a big placenta while the other's was small, or if their umbilical cords were different widths, that could be enough of a difference to change what should be nearly identical genetics.

It's the chicken or the egg. Did the intrauterine environment (nurture) lead to the changes in the genes (nature)? Or did a genetic issue of the mother (nature) lead to an issue in the intrauterine environment (nurture)? Did the changes in genes happen due to the landscapes in which the boys were raised, or was there something within the DNA of the boys that influenced the environment and then prompted the difference? DNA shapes who we are, and thus our environment. Likewise, the environment in which we live shapes our DNA. There's no nature versus nurture debate. There's only a nature and nurture ouroboros.[8]

With the twin examples, we can see very clearly that the environments we find ourselves a part of aren't always random. The Jims didn't end up on Florida vacations purely by chance. Our environments are absolutely shaped *by* us, the proclivities and propensities encoded in our genes helping to dictate the environments we find ourselves in, which then put us in settings and situations that turn around and impact our entire body system. You're born with certain traits, such as temperament, that influence the way you interact with your environment and thus how your environment interacts with you. A calm baby elicits a different parental attitude than a fussy one, which then, in turn, creates a household that shapes what kind of child that baby will become. Someone born with a high tolerance for risk may choose to live in a crowded big city, while someone with a low tolerance for risk might choose the comforts of a small town where everyone knows everyone. Someone born with an innate ability to excel at a sport might go where they can play that sport, whereas someone with an academic pursuit might live only where their specific subject of knowledge can be in focus.

And then those environments influence us, with their varying levels of stress, pollution, access to nutrition, and opportunities for all kinds of risk and reward alike—all things that can act as musicians to turn on or off our genes. And the genes, influenced

---

[8]The ouroboros is an ancient symbol of a serpent or dragon eating its own tail and represents infinity or a never-ending cycle.

by our environment, affect both minor and vital functions—even someone's internal protection levels against illnesses like cancer. Where you live and who you keep as company, all of those things change us at our very core.

As in the case of Scott Kelly, some epigenetic changes can be reversed. But some of them can't. Instead, they "imprint."[9] To geneticists, imprinting occurs when one of a gene's two alleles is permanently silenced by an epigenetic process.

Time for another quick science lesson!

Each gene in your chromosome (remember, this is the partial recipe from your DNA that is in each cell and that tells each cell what it's supposed to do) exists twice—one copy from each parent. The copies are not necessarily the same—such as in genes for hair color, where the gene from your mother might be for blond hair and the one from your father is for black hair—and the differences between the two genes are known as *alleles*. A given gene may have multiple different possible alleles, but only two alleles are present in any individual. For example, a person with type AB blood has one allele for A and one for B. For this person, type O (which is also a possible allele for blood type) does not exist within their chromosome. When one allele is "turned on" due to epigenetics, it can silence the other allele—say, the gene from your mom for being short silencing the gene from your dad for being tall. But in epigenetic imprinting, this silencing becomes permanent, meaning it's both irreversible in you *and* gets passed on to your children.

By silencing certain information, these imprinted genes alter the way DNA is passed down to offspring. It's basically as if, instead of

---

[9] You will find many places in this book where the term *imprint* is used by some person or another. I, through some cosmic mojo, named this book well before I started putting it together. It was a wonderful surprise, when researching the book, to find how so many people used this term to describe aspects of what I feel is in the Imprint. Sometimes, I truly believe, the universe tells its own tales

letting the roulette wheel of your DNA determine whether you'll get the blond or black hair from your mother's and father's genes, the imprinting silences the black-haired gene so that you *only* get the chance to be blond. In the case of hair color, that might not seem too terrifying. But the information being passed down to you through genes is vast, including everything from how your metabolism should function to whether you should fear water, so a permanent silencing of one gene to promote another can be helpful, such as when the switched-on gene gives you a strength to overcome an adversity, such as an immunity to types of cancer, or hurtful, as when the switched-on gene is damaged or increases risks and vulnerabilities, such as a weak heart. And the likelihood of you having at least one silenced allele is high, because researchers have identified a couple hundred human genes that can be imprinted, and posit there could be close to six hundred or more.

In ancient times, elders would enrapture their communities through the sharing of their memories and wisdom. They spun tales and told stories that conveyed an expanse of information about how to exist and even thrive in their shared culture. Their oral traditions touched on everything from ethics to history to survival. This passing down of information ensured the experiences of the past were salient and memorable for those in the present, enabling their young to go forward into the world, seemingly more prepared.

In a way, similar "memories" from your parents are told to you through imprinted genes. This imprinted memory gives our DNA information that directly reflects experiences that occurred in the lives of our parents. Something happened that created an epigenetic response in our parents' genes, and an echo of that response is then imprinted on us, whispered in our own cells. But you have to wonder what information actually lives in these memories we're receiving from these imprinted genes. And if, as Joshua Foer states in *Moonwalking with Einstein*, "Who we are and what we do is fundamentally a function of what we remember" (p. 67), how are those memories influencing who we are?

Julia

Julia and Bill are sitting on opposite ends of the couch. Her arms are folded and she stares toward the door, while Bill stares at me, a pleading look in his eye. After weeks of sessions filled with heightened emotions, the silence in the room feels out of place.

Julia had opened the session with a recap of a call she had the night before. "I was talking to Mom after a fight Bill and I had," Julia stated. "She started taking his side and I just got so mad. Like, *how could she?* I'm her daughter! And then . . ."

She trailed off for a minute, and as I looked to Bill and then back to her, I sensed something new was about to unfold.

She restarted.

"You have to understand, my parents had *the* best relationship. At least to me."

And I steady myself for where I know this is heading.

Julia and Bill came to see me after struggling through years of trouble in their relationship, including several bouts of infidelity on Julia's part. Julia had always asserted that the root cause of the infidelity was the troubles between her and Bill, and that if the relationship were better she wouldn't have the desire to have a relationship outside of her marriage. With a commitment to working on their issues in session, she was stalwart in her assertion she would never cheat again. Now the revelation by Julia's mother threatened to absolutely shatter any hope for reconciliation.

Julia continues. "They were so loving, and like, I never thought anything was wrong. But apparently not," she spits, the anger seething from her. "*Apparently*, my father had cheated on my mom, like, a *lot*. All the way up until he died! We're talking *dozens* of relationships," she seethes. "I never knew."

After a minute, Bill speaks.

"What am I supposed to do with this?" he asks. "She's been the one who doesn't trust me—*me!*—even though I've told her time and time again that I'm not that kind of person. I come from good people, I'm a good person. And now, this."

I watch as Julia deflates, a look of resignation on her face.

"She's gonna be just like him," Bill asserts, both anger and sadness filling his tone. "She was always acting like I was the trigger. But it's her. It's in her damn blood."

With lament, Julia whispers, "But I never fucking knew."

5

Hidden Memories

For those of us
who were imprinted with fear
like a faint line in the center of our foreheads
learning to be afraid with our mother's milk
for by this weapon
this illusion of some safety to be found
the heavy-footed hoped to silence us
For all of us
this instant and this triumph
We were never meant to survive.

—AUDRE LORDE, "A LITANY FOR SURVIVAL"

Scientists first observed memories being passed from parent to offspring while studying plants. They named this phenomenon transgenerational epigenetic inheritance and it's been a game changer ever since (Hughes, 2014). Plants, it seems, take memories about what it takes to survive in their environment and epigenetically pass down that knowledge to their seedlings. For instance, tomatoes pass along information about what time of year their seedlings should ripen in order to best survive. And maize passes down to its seedlings preferred kernel colors, which I can only assume happens because it's a color that gets eaten more at that location, thus spreading maize out and about through the wonders of corn poop? I need a corn expert to help out on that one.

Regardless of the *why* though, the maize inheritance raised some additional eyebrows because the maize plant is basically the identical twin of the plant world. Maize has mirror-image DNA, which means all maize *should* be exactly the same. But like the forced blond situation we discussed in an earlier chapter, an epigenetic change occurs that overrides the identical DNA code and sends information to seedlings to be the chosen color instead. And in fact, it will send that mandate down through hundreds of generations.

After the plant findings, memory inheritance research just took off. Scientists everywhere started looking in all corners of the world for these passed down memories and have been successful at almost every turn. We now have evidence that the phenomenon occurs in all kinds of organisms, including humans. And that's where the science gets really cool. For instance, did you know that water fleas exposed to the scent of a predator send information to their children to ensure those offspring come from the womb (so to speak) with the armor necessary to protect against that threat? And researchers found that mice parents exposed to altered diets, low temperatures, or toxins had pups with behavioral changes that indicated *they* were the ones in those situations, not their parents, even though the kids were never exposed to those stimuli. Did you ever see *The Princess Bride*? In it, on a quest to avenge true love, Westley outsmarts one of his opponents by slowly building an immunity to a poison called iocane. If what occurred with the water fleas and mice happened to Westley, Westley's and Buttercup's children would be born with immunity to iocane (or at least with a way to detect it), purely as a result of their parents' experience.

Evolutionarily speaking, especially in the case of physical characteristics such as a natural defense against a toxin, this inheritance makes sense. Giving offspring traits to survive a particular environmental hazard would certainly be helpful in a species making it in the long term. And you'll find a lot of what's out there in published epigenetics research today focuses on exactly that—the physical manifestations and health ramifications we incur as a result of challenges within our parents' environment. Yet as with all things, we get both the good *and* the bad. A wide variety of illnesses and health issues, both physical and mental, show up as a result of your parents' passed down memories. You currently can find studies showing how epigenetic inheritance affects mental, respiratory, cardiovascular, reproductive, and neurobehavioral systems within the body, in addition to influencing risks related to autoimmune diseases and almost all types of cancer (Weinhold, 2006).

But we are more than just a heart and lungs. We also are thoughts and emotions, behavior and intuition. We are more complex than words can adequately describe. So if there's evidence that information is being passed down to us that affects our physical makeup, wouldn't it be conceivable that other information—related to thoughts and behavior—also comes along for the ride?

Of course it is.

Inclinations and penchants, wants and desires—all of these have been discovered written on your genetic code. For example, a study by Salvatore et al. (2018) found that an individual's chance of divorce was heavily dependent on genetic factors, with adopted children having divorce histories that more closely mirrored that of their biological families—specifically of their biological fathers—than of their adoptive families. And a 2019 study found that owning a dog was based on a greater than 50% predisposition from your ancestors (Fall et al., 2019).

Before I go on, I want to pause to highlight the term *ancestors* here. This is an important distinction for us while looking at our Imprint. It's important for us to know that some of the epigenetic studies trace these generational hand-me-downs through *centuries*. For instance, in worms, they've found an exposure to high temperatures passed related memories down through fourteen generations (Klosin et al., 2017). Most people can't get their Ancestry.com tree to go back that far, and here a bodily response to a high temperature from fourteen generations ago is still being carried out. And some research on worms found that turned-off genes remained silenced for eighty—*eighty!*—generations or more (Curry, 2019). Now *that's* a dynasty. But OK, that's worms. What about multigenerational impact in humans?

Human studies in epigenetic inheritance are . . . tricky. Why? Because of the same issues we talked about that make the nature versus nurture discussions challenging. First and foremost, it's hard to remove the effect of parenting—to disentangle what comes through growing up in your house from what might be passed down in your DNA. Like, did a military vet's experiences of being in combat epigenetically affect their offspring, passing down memories that triggered behavior in their kids? Or did the experience of warfare make that vet a really crappy parent, and it's the crappy parenting that's actually influencing their children's behaviors?

My grandmother was an orphan during the Depression. Like many children who struggled during that time and had so little when she was growing up, as an adult, she basically hoarded food. This woman would cook so much food at family gatherings, you'd think she had been assigned meal duty for all of northern Ohio. She had three refrigerators and two freezers, and her basement could rival a fallout shelter with the amount of canned goods stocked down there. Holidays at her house were *lit*. A table filled with pies and cakes and different meats and like 280 different sides (that may be only a *slight* exaggeration). When she died and we were going through her pantry, many of the canned foods had expired years before. *Expired canned food*, people. Do you know how old canned food has to be to expire?!

Now, in *my* childhood home, the home of my gram's son—my father? There was no overflowing pantry. We ate simple meals, and holiday feasts were sufficient but reserved. (In truth, I don't remember even a single holiday meal at our house growing up, but there was a picture of a turkey and some sides once, so clearly it must have happened.) We did not buy food unnecessarily, but we also did *not* waste food in our house.

One time, my sister and I *real-l-ly* wanted this *E.T.* cereal and my father, pretty much antifrivolity during that stage of my life, finally caved, but only with the stipulation that we must eat all of it before he would buy another box of cereal. And this is when I learned that the breakfast gods aren't always fair. The *E.T.* cereal was, according to my sister, me, and possibly millions of other kids since it was only on the shelves for one year, abhorrent. Some vomit-inducing mix of what someone thought peanut butter *should* taste like and a burned orange encased in sugarless chocolate. Straight inedible. And so, after the first heaping bowl, neither my sister nor I could stomach it enough to eat it. After a week or two, many other parents would have replaced the box of cereal. Not my father. Weeks and perhaps months went by and that box of death flexed hard atop our refrigerator like the Eye of Sauron, taunting us with each visit to the kitchen. The cereal went stale well before my father eventually caved and bought us another box of cereal. Shredded Wheat. The sensible, steadfast, nonfrivolous choice.

And that's the trouble we run into when we look at human epigenetic studies. Did the psychological impact of growing up with a parent who was so seemingly uneconomical about food shape my father's extremely frugal behavior? Or was it epigenetic whispers passed down to him about the scarcity environment she had experienced, warning him to not be wasteful? It's simply not clear.

And then there's this second complexity to human studies. Research on intergenerational transfer takes, per the name, generations. Decades and centuries have to pass in order to study the outcomes of parenting and in utero environments, and frankly most studies don't have the budget or the patience or the literal lives needed to wait that long. That's why animal research is so abundant. You simply don't need to wait. Mice? Those buggers reach adulthood in about three months, making study of the impact of genes versus environment much more accessible. And what's coming out of those studies is worthy of our collective focus.

A quick pop out to note that, for some of you, these studies might be distressing to read. Using animals in research is not without harm, and I personally find it difficult to justify the ends using those means. I could not be cruel to any creature for the sake of learning. That said, these studies have occurred and do exist, so if you're able to read on, please do. Let us learn what we can from them.

In 2001, Isabelle Mansuy of the University of Zurich and ETH Zurich separated mouse moms (we'll call them group A) from their pups (group B). The separation itself was taxing to the animals, but on top of that, the researchers full-on traumatized the moms by confining some in tubes and continuously dropping others in water with no way to get to safety (Curry, 2019). The mothers were eventually returned to their homes, but by that point, they were frantic, distracted, and distressed, unable to properly mother their pups and in some cases ignoring them outright. For their part, the pups had already been pretty stressed because they had to deal with the whole missing mom situation. But now adding in a mom who wouldn't or couldn't tend to their needs was too much, and physical analysis confirmed that the pups too were now traumatized, according to markers—such as stress hormones—that scientists use in the lab for this diagnosis.

Unsurprisingly (and just like what would happen in humans), when those traumatized group B pups grew up, they acted in unhealthy, sometimes harmful ways—the opposite of mice who are raised in nonstressful, healthy environments. But the reason we're talking about them on these pages is because of what happened to the B pups' eventual offspring.

The group B mice had some pups (group C). These grandchildren of the originally traumatized mothers displayed the same unhealthy and harmful behaviors as their parents. And you might think, *Well yeah, their parents were traumatized children.* But hold your horses. The research team then took happy, untraumatized female mice and had them breed with the group B male pups, and then removed the group B pups so that they couldn't be bad dads. We'll call these single-mom-raised babies group D.

The researchers then went ahead and split up the group D pups into different environments—none of which held any of the group B or C mice—and let them live out their little mouse lives. The scientists repeated this process many times, going as far out as six generations, separating offspring and ensuring they were being raised in different environments, unexposed to any of the original group B or C mice. And what they found is unnerving. There were cellular changes that mimicked those of the originally traumatized mice in *each* of the six subsequent generations, even though none of these later mice had direct contact with their traumatized ancestors. In essence, the memory of trauma was passed down to the mice, not through stories or even observed behavior but coded into their DNA.

Descendants of the traumatized mice exhibited both molecular changes (like the changes in Scott the astronaut) and *behavioral* changes. For instance, just as we see in some human trauma survivors, the trauma-descendant mice displayed more risk-taking behavior, such as hanging out too close to the edge of a high platform. But what's mind-blowing is that the mice didn't just display the typical type of behavior that might come from having had childhood trauma, despite not having had any. They also behaved as if *they* were the ones who had been dropped in water or confined in tubes—physical echoes of their great-great-great-great-great-grandmother.

Mice with no previous exposure to repeatedly almost drowning fight when placed in water. They try to swim to safety. It would take multiple drops in water and multiple subsequent failures for those mice to give up, which is what happened to those first mothers. It takes multiple brushes with death for them to give up trying to survive. And yet the very first time the sixth-generation pups were exposed to being placed in water, they went into a full meltdown and "gave up," as if they knew immediately there was no chance of attempting to swim to safety.

What's more, this diminished survival response—in mice as in humans—is an indicator of a depressive state. These mice, who had nothing outwardly problematic occur in their lives, were born both traumatized and with an inclination to depression. Born with a memory that made a single dip into water actually one event in a string of traumatizing moments—the knowledge of defeat, of hopelessness, already learned.

But again, we get the good with the bad. Nematodes are worms that, like many of us during the COVID epidemic, only leave the safety of their home in order to find food (Schuster, 2019). These little creatures don't have eyes, and they have to rely solely on their sense of smell to notice, identify, and then go find food. Being a blind, yummy breakfast for birds makes going out of the house a huge risk, so the nematode brain creates a whole group of RNA, copies of DNA containing instructions, that coordinate cells like a military war room to ensure odor detection is spot on. This group of RNA makes the call on whether it's worth the risk to leave shelter and go find whatever it is they're smelling. Any nematodes that can't make this critical RNA have defective food identification skills and eventually die.

In June 2019, a bunch of these nematodes were studied to see if they would be able to pass down this odor detection skill to their offspring (Blum, 2020). Nematode regeneration time is just three and a half days, which makes seeing what gets passed down through generations a super quick process. Plus, every worm produces a crap ton of babies, and if hundreds of your kids have the same genetic memory, it decreases the likelihood that chance had anything to do with a result. And because nematodes fertilize themselves, differences in DNA among children are minimal because there's no second-parent genes to choose from. It's basically the equivalent of having, like, three hundred identical twins.

The study results showed that, when the worm's mother had the necessary RNA group to pull off the odor detection war room, their progeny could successfully determine when to seek out food—*even if the worm itself didn't have the RNA biology.* What's more, this ghosted "Should I leave the house and forage?" skill passed down through at least three generations. Which means great-grandchildren inherited a skill even when they didn't have the actual hardware in their cellular structure that's needed to have that skill. That's *crazy*. It's the ability to taste all the things your great-grandmother ate, even if you don't have taste buds.

Now you might think, OK fine. It makes sense that survival-based information would somehow make its way down to offspring. That

ensures the survival of the species. But surely nonessential information wouldn't make the journey? Well, in another study, Larry Feig
at Tufts University stressed out a whole different bunch of mice,
this time male. Instead of making them fear for their lives, Feig's
team focused on stressful but not traumatizing experiences. For
instance, they routinely changed out the other mice in their study
mice's cages (Curry, 2019). If you don't think that sounds stressful,
imagine how you'd feel if you woke up every day and your world
consisted of an entirely different cast of characters. Feig found the
stressed-out males' sperm had alterations in some sncRNA[10] groups,
which appeared to make their offspring more anxious and less
sociable than the pups of the other, unstressed mice. What's more,
the anxious, less sociable outcome for offspring occurred even if the
fathers' stress occurred not just in the time surrounding conception
but also in the months before.

Scientists have been spending a whole lot of time lately trying
to figure out where these inherited memories are coming from. Researcher Jennifer Chan took Feig's experiment and tried to break it
down further. Instead of looking directly at sperm, Chan focused on
a group of cells that help sperm develop into their final state (Landhuis, 2018). These cells secrete tiny blister-looking things called vesicles that fuse together with sperm cells, sharing information related
to environment. Chan collected sperm from a single male mouse
that had never experienced stress and put half of his sperm in a dish
with vesicles that had been exposed to stress hormones. The other
half of sperm sat with vesicles that were all peace, love, and Zen.
Both sets of sperm were then placed into nonstressed females, and
I'm really hoping by now you can guess what happened. The pups
from the nonstress-exposed sperm developed normally. But pups

---

[10] Cells contain short strands of noncoding RNA—sncRNA—that act like mischievous children, either
interfering with or amping up the job the RNA is trying to get cells to do.

who came from sperm that was simply exposed to stressed vesicles showed the same abnormal stress response as the mice descended from Feig's batch of stressed dads.

And in 2018, scientists at UCLA replicated transferred memories between snails, only this time, they used RNA injections instead of relying on offspring (McFarling and STAT, 2018). The researchers shocked snails until they had a learned response to those shocks, then injected the shocked snail's RNA into random, unrelated, fully healthy snails. And you guessed it. The injected snails began to exhibit the same response to stimuli that the shocked snails did, as if they had the memory of being shocked themselves. What's more, this type of research has been replicated time and time again. They've given male mice and worms and flies altered diets and trauma and even exposed them to illicit substances. No matter what, memories of those experiences make their way to their children—and often to many generations afterwards.

* * *

Most people are other people. Their thoughts are someone else's opinions, their lives a mimicry, their passions a
quotation.

—OSCAR WILDE, *DE PROFUNDIS*

Despite the complexity involved in human studies, we do have a
few to look at. It's important to note that epigenetics as a specific
field of study has only been around since the 1940s, and in those
early years, the research relied heavily on looking at medical literature and already established data. High-quality, in-depth human
studies have only been around since roughly the 2000s (Deichmann,
2016). But even with such a short span of research, one thing is
pretty clear: stressed-out and traumatized parents leave invisible
scars on their children.

One of epigenetics' earliest human findings centered on the
effects of the "Dutch hunger winter," a famine that fell upon the
Netherlands in 1944. The lack of food that winter capped years of
struggle already encountered as a result of World War II and thus
was considered a supremely stressful period to be alive. When epigenetic researchers reviewed the medical literature encompassing
those years, they discovered that women who were pregnant during
the famine had children who died earlier than children born just
before the famine, even though they were both born during the
other struggles related to the war. What's more, the children born
during the famine also had higher rates of obesity, diabetes, and
schizophrenia.

Further medical reviews indicated that heart disease is more
prevalent in people whose parents had food insecurity as children,
even if the food insecurity only occurred while the child was in the

womb—a perhaps medically relevant fact for those people whose parents grew up during the Depression. And historical records show the sons of men who were prisoners of war during the Civil War were more likely to die early than the sons of veterans who were not POWs.

Certainly, a mother's womb during famine could be a pretty awful environment. And because germ cells develop in the fetus, it's possible that the intrauterine environment was overly inhospitable and *that's* what caused the generational impact, not some passed down memory happening within the cells. As I've said before, scientists only start to really link something as epigenetic inheritance if they see an impact that stems from completely unexposed generations, as we saw with the mice. And though that type of research has only begun to take shape in the past twenty years, there's some indications that memories truly are the culprit.

Research currently under way on a group of Pakistani orphans is showing similarities to the traumatized mice experiment. Though this study will take decades to fully complete, they have already documented changes in some of the orphans' sncRNA and levels of fatty acids in blood and saliva—indicators of trauma experience (Curry, 2019). The researchers will now wait to see if those changes show up in the next generation.

As we peer into this grey, we might see how these findings could raise some concerns if we pull too hard on what's there. For instance, if mice can be induced into a depressive state due to exposure to a traumatic stimuli they never experienced, what does this mean with regard to a possible cause for depression in humans? How do we know we're depressed because *we* are depressed? What if the depression we're facing is at least in some ways the ghost of someone else's experiences? A response to events that happened decades or even centuries ago? If children of POWs die earlier than children of other vets, what does this mean about our policies related to war?

Should those who send men and women to war provide help (such as health care) to the children of those soldiers to counter the effects we know exist? How much of what we're experiencing and suffering from today truly a result of our own doing and how much is a relic of what happened to those before us? Our anxiety, our depression, our fears, our desires . . . how much is *truly* ours?

* * *

Maybe the journey isn't so much about becoming anything. Maybe it's about un-becoming everything that isn't
really you.

—PAUL COELHO

For information to make it from one generation to the next,
memories would need to survive multiple rounds of rigorous cleansing and reprogramming. In humans, the first cleanse happens just
hours after conception, when most gene expression is stripped from
an embryo. Then, as the embryo develops and divides and cells begin
to turn into various tissue types, that stripping happens again. What
this is *supposed* to be doing is setting you up to have your own gene
expression rather than being an exact clone of your parents. If your
parents had brown eyes, it's because brown eyes were what was expressed in their genes. But instead of that expression dictating your
eye color, your genes are scrubbed to allow the roulette wheel to
give you what you got. My sister got my parents' brown, I got blue.
It's a way to give you your own unique combination of features and
characteristics. Your own clean slate. And this attempt to remove
influence is, like, really hard-core. While you're still in utero, the
cells that are slated to become *your* sperm or eggs (so, your future
kid maker) undergo yet another round of scrubbing, designed to
ensure that even if something of your parents escaped the cleansing
and ended up in you, there's no chance in hell it's gonna pass down
to *your* kids.

Yet despite all that purging, memories are escaping. Imprinted
genes slide and sneak into your program. Sarah Kimmins, an epi-
geneticist trying to understand imprinted genes, stated, "There is
a growing consensus that there are more regions than previously

thought that escape reprogramming" (Hughes, 2014). And I think that's saying something. You start with all this knowledge that's supposed to be wiped clean—a whiteboard that's meant to be erased. But there's information that clearly wants to be passed on—something that defies what's "supposed" to happen. We can still see the erased outline of ink on our whiteboard's surface. A biological process that's meant to make us forget where we came from, doesn't. The history is still there, ghosts of the past embedded in our cells. As I mentioned earlier, they've identified *hundreds* of genes that have been imprinted. And I suspect, with regard to what's getting passed down from parent to child, there's still more for us to uncover than just what's in our DNA.

* * *

Nothing of me is original. I am the combined effort of everyone I've ever known.

—CHUCK PALAHNIUK, *INVISIBLE MONSTERS*

In 1953, a professor at the Department of Psychiatry at Stanford University School of Medicine named Josephine Hilgard described what she called "anniversary reactions." Hilgard wrote that people experienced psychosis and depression at the same age that a traumatic incident (death, accident, and so on) had occurred for their parent. Furthermore, people sometimes developed other health issues—such as pneumonia or headaches—that were uncannily identical to experiences their parents had at that same age. A parent's life, replicated in their child. And it's not just in our physiological systems that this echo seems to occur.

Rachel Yehuda, a professor of psychiatry and the neuroscience of trauma, opened a clinic in 1993, hoping to help Holocaust victims with their trauma. However, the clinic was flooded with inquiries not from Holocaust victims but from the grown children of survivors (Paul, 2010). These second-generation family members were seeking treatment because *they* were experiencing trauma symptoms, despite not encountering traumatic events themselves. Yehuda noticed that these family members were indeed experiencing symptoms that echoed the post-traumatic stress disorder (PTSD) symptoms of their parents who survived.

But in an eerie surprise, the family members were also experiencing something Yehuda could never have anticipated. These adult children of Holocaust survivors were reporting having nightmares —dreams of the same exact type reported by survivors. These nightmares, Yehuda explained, are where a survivor is "chased, persecuted, tortured or annihilated, as if they were re-living the Second World War over and over again" (Kellermann, 2013). Such a nightmare is to be expected in a person reliving the event. But how was it possible that these second-generation family members were also having these dreams, despite not having witnessed the Holocaust? What's more, the nightmares occurred even in adult children whose parents didn't discuss their traumas during the Holocaust, whether because they were unwilling or were unable to provide any details. Refusing to dismiss the findings they were seeing (as many scientists might have), Yehuda's team noted it was as if these second-generation family members "inherited the unconscious minds of their parents."

We have a connection with our ancestors—a deep one—and what has "escaped reprogramming" isn't just in your genes. If our ancestors are able to slip past our reprogramming to pass down traits, behaviors, and even memories, what else could they be doing? Are there other ways they might be influencing us? The mother ship, sending signals to its fleet?

The entirety of our identity is not fully accounted for by our DNA and the environments we live in. There are other origins for the Imprint, our true intergenerational inheritance, if we only pay attention to what's outside the limitations of what we "know." If we allow ourselves to dig deeper still.

Chris

As he takes his seat, Chris remarks rather casually, "I haven't felt well for days."

Chris, a forty-four-year-old male who works in IT, is more at ease now than when he initially came to see me several months ago. At the beginning of our work together, Chris viewed himself as very type A, leaning heavily on his analytical capabilities for just about everything. So when he found himself in a depressive state that no amount of logic or reasoning seemed to relieve, he reached out for help. Just over a month before this current moment in time, Chris had told me about a situation that shifted our work together, and ultimately how he saw himself. It was his first tangible insight into his Imprint.

Chris's father was in the military and was deployed during Chris's eleventh-grade year. About two months after his father's deployment, Chris became ill and was eventually diagnosed with shingles—a surprise to his family and the doctors as Chris was otherwise healthy and shingles mostly effects the elderly and those with compromised immune systems. Seeing it in healthy young people is a rarity. When Chris's father called a week later to check in, everyone was surprised to find out that exactly that same week and over six thousand miles away, Chris's father had also been diagnosed with shingles.

Given the time they'd been apart, I remarked that the two could not have contracted it from one another. But with his analytic side dominating, Chris dismissed the incident as coincidence. When I asked him to humor me and introduced to him the concept of the Imprint, Chris started to see his mere coincidence turn into something uncanny.

As we dug deeper, he began to see a pattern in other mysterious "coincidences" that had occurred. While he was in his twenties, Chris and his mother had been diagnosed with mono within weeks of one another, despite being separated by hundreds of miles and not being in close contact with each other for more than a year. And then there were the times that Chris would experience bouts of unexplainable ailments or phantom pains, only to get word from a sibling, aunt, or cousin shortly thereafter that they had been experiencing health issues that corresponded with Chris's experience.

Using the Imprint, Chris now looked at his connections when he encountered an ailment rather than simply looking in the medicine cabinet. The viewpoint expanded his narrative of the experience of sickness and pain into one that held meaning other than that there was simply a weakness within his own body.

"Whoever's sick needs to get better soon, because I'm so over it," he quipped lightheartedly.

And sure enough, Chris was right. Within a week of our meeting, he found that he was once again experiencing a parallel medical path with a parent. Talking on the phone, still hundreds of miles apart, Chris and his mother realized they were both experiencing the exact same symptoms, and what's more, had unknowingly scheduled the same procedure to deal with those symptoms—a procedure set to happen on the exact same day at the exact same time.

6

⟨꙰⟩

Spooky Action

What we do now echoes in eternity.

—MARCUS AURELIUS, *Meditations*

In the 1998 movie *Practical Magic*, there's a scene where women gather to help the town witches perform a spell. As they prepare, one of the helpers says, "Once, I was across town, my daughter had a nightmare. I swear, I could hear her crying." To which one of the witches retorts, "There's a little witch in all of us." Turns out, she was right. Beyond the realm of fiction, the experience of preternaturally sensing when a loved one is experiencing something, whether it be pain or joy or even death, has occurred throughout history.

In the late 1800s, Bishop Samuel Wilberforce, a respected clergyman and high-standing public speaker, was in his library. He was with his clergy, doing whatever it is that clergy do, when Wilberforce suddenly exclaimed, "I am certain that something has happened to one of my sons" (Ashwell, 1880, p. 397). In a time before phones, internet, or any sort of swift communication, the clergy bustled around him, presuming perhaps that he was experiencing some sort of delusional fever as his oldest son was very much out to sea at that time. Yet it was discovered later that at about the moment that the bishop was making his abrupt proclamation, his son was indeed in the throes of having an accident in which his foot was crushed.

During the siege of Multan in 1848, one of the generals was severely wounded. As he lay there preparing for his own death, the general requested that his wedding ring be removed and sent to his wife (Leadbeater, 1918). At about that same moment but some 150 miles away, that same general's wife was reported to have been over-taken with a vision. She claimed she saw her husband being taken off the field, death imminent. What's more, she claimed to have heard in her vision, and in the general's voice, his request to have the ring sent to her.

And in 2013, Today.com featured stories from several mothers who had followed their "mother's intuition" and swore there had been a psychic connection (Brasfield, 2013). One of the mothers, Andrea Alley, suddenly felt the overwhelming need to get to her son as quickly as possible, only to find upon arrival that her son had experienced a bloody accident just moments before.

These types of stories hint at a connection between us that's much deeper than many thought possible. An unseen pull and tug of the bodies, thoughts, and emotions of connected people. As if we, like tree roots, are entwined, bound in our lives together. It doesn't matter if you believe these connections result from magic or psychic abilities or you chock it all up to coincidence, like all of the seemingly unbelievable things in the world, there is a truth tucked in it somewhere.

We know that the myth of werewolves is likely based on the condition of hypertrichosis, or excessive hair growth anywhere on the body. We know that the concept of vampires originated either from folks of yore not understanding how decomposition works or observing porphyria disorder (Maas and Voets, 2014). And we know that the zombie tales of the seventeenth and eighteenth centuries were a true-to-life metaphor for the enslaved in Haiti—people experiencing a "death" of their freedom and autonomy over their own bodies and minds, forced into a lifeless existence of never-ending misery and oppression (Mariani, 2015). And so it is that the uncanny things that occur as a seemingly supernatural connection between people are no different. There is truth in the tales—we just have to be open to finding it. And perhaps the field of quantum mechanics can help.

***

Quantum entanglement refers to two particles with mass and energy, like atoms, that are linked together and act like a single system, despite being physically separated from each other (Popkin, 2018). The linkage occurs in part due to the law of conservation of energy, which (if you recall sixth-grade science class) states that energy can't be created or destroyed, only moved from one thing to another. So let's say you have a particle, and that particle contains one hundred units of energy. You split that particle in two and you and a friend each take a piece. Let's say your piece contains thirty of the original hundred units of energy. The law of conservation of energy says that your friend's portion would then have to contain the remaining seventy units, since the energy between the two always has to add up to the original hundred. Make sense?

Where it gets interesting is if your friend's particle, say, goes on a diet and reduces its energy to sixty units. Also from our sixth-grade science class, we know that energy can't be destroyed, only transferred, which means the ten units of energy your friend's particle lost has to go *somewhere*. Now, since both your and your friend's pieces were originally from the same single particle, they are, in the language of quantum science, entangled. Despite being physically separated from one another, entangled pieces act as a single system, a whole. So your particle becomes that "somewhere." Those ten units need a home, and in a fairy godmother moment, there's a cosmic bibbidi-bobbidi-boo and voilà! Your piece now has forty units of energy.

Quantum entanglement is not just relegated to theory. In 2018, Simon Gröblacher and his colleagues etched light beams into silicon chips and separated them (Riedinger et al., 2018). Using lasers, Gröblacher's team added energy to make the light on one of the beams vibrate. But though they focused their lasers only on one beam, both beams were affected. As with our particle scenario, the information they added to the one impacted both. Another team, led by researcher Mika Sillanpää, manufactured super-duper miniature disks and placed them on a silicon chip (Popkin, 2018). They used microwaves to make one of the disks move, and again, the entangled pieces acted as one. Both disks moved even when only one disk was given the ability to do so. And what's more, their entanglement could last indefinitely.

And in 2021, scientists surmised that animals can sense earth's magnetic poles due to quantum entanglement, which then affects their behaviors (McCray, 2021). One of the things we know the magnetic pole impacts is a bird's ability to successfully navigate migratory patterns, and the researchers wondered whether humans could have behaviors as a result of this same effect, we just don't consciously recognize it. As one researcher noted, "The joyous thing about this research is to see that the relationship between the spins of two individual electrons can have a major effect on biology," meaning, the entanglement of the magnetic pole and the cells within animals can drastically influence the behavior of whatever, or whoever, is entangled. And it's not just energy that gets passed across distances. Entangled particles also share *information* with each other—data that could influence your behavior. And what's more, they can do it instantaneously, as if they were still united, instead of being miles, or even galaxies, apart (Conover, 2019).

Albert Einstein called the instantaneous communication of entangled particles "spooky action at a distance." In spooky action, if a particle changes, any other particles that are entangled with it will instantly change themselves to match. And according to Einstein, that distance part? It can be light-years. In a nutshell, that's like if you were a particle (which technically you are, because you're made up of millions of them) and read a recipe while cooking stew in Maine, an entangled twin sibling of yours that was living on Mars would learn that same recipe at the exact same time, without having to look up a thing. What's more, the "information" we're talking about can include a whole litany of things, including the experiences of our very own five senses.

On December 17, 1888, there was a news story in the *Columbus Enquirer-Sun* about a man named Frank Bangart. Poor Frank had his hand cut off while working at his job as a brakeman for the Central Railroad, and in an "everyone knows this is how a horror movie starts" moment, they buried Frank's hand. Of course, within days of the burial, Frank began to complain that his buried hand was hurting him and needed to be adjusted. And the man must've been channeling some serious two-year-old tantrum energy, because after what I can only imagine was a *wh-o-o-le* lot of cursing by the authorities, they agreed to dig up, adjust, and then rebury Frank's hand.

Alas, after some time, Frank once again began to complain about feeling the phantom pain of his now twice-buried severed hand. Frank stated he felt pain because when they adjusted it the first time, authorities had made it so his little finger was "lapped over the third finger." And sure enough, when they dug the hand up this time (because apparently they did, and I seriously have so many questions about why), they indeed found the fingers were crossed as

Frank had felt. They straightened the fingers and, for the third time, reburied the hand.

There is no more written on the subject, so we're left to wonder whether Frank felt pain from his buried hand again. But his story, and frankly the whole concept of phantom limb syndrome, is very aligned with Einstein's spooky action. Historically, researchers have assumed that the sensations of feeling missing body parts was nerve malfunction. But a paper written as recently as 2022 about phantom limb syndrome summated, "The underlying pathophysiology remains poorly understood" (Hanyu-Deutmeyer et al., 2023). And perhaps this poor understanding is because researchers are looking for an explanation all from Process, without Nuance. After all, if a separated particle can send energy and information to its once connected parts across galaxies of distance, then it doesn't seem like much of a stretch that a disconnected body part—once a part of a whole—is sending information back to its body.

To further get spooky, quantum effects are so sensitive they can react within the lightest of signals, such as gravitational waves. That means information can be shared not only across distances but also across time. And when you add the concept of time crystals—particles that are perpetually in motion and never rest—into the mix, we now have the possibility of information and memory sharing that is everlasting.

Every human, you included, starts as a single embryo. The egg and sperm that kicked off the creation of you contain loads and loads of genetic material—thus, particles—from your parents and from who knows what other ancestors. Thus, particles from your ancestors are entangled with *you*. You contain a literal part of your parents, which contains a literal part of their parents, which in a perpetual nesting doll situation, contains particles of every ancestor you've ever had. You are merely the split-off forty units, so to speak. And that means that any information that the whole knows, you know. And since information among entangled particles is shared instantaneously and across time, the entangled particles that make up you, that are from your grandmother, your mother, your great-great-grandfather—at least some of their life, their memories, are also in you. All the information from all your ancestors is still here, energy and information just transferred, divided among the remaining entangled parts. And as people die, that information, that energy, having to be transferred, just keeps getting passed.

It's the same as you and your friend splitting that particle. If you have living parents or grandparents, their particles are still entangled with you, sharing energy. Sharing information. Because your particles, the goo that makes up you, is still tied to them, entwined. Imprints of connection that persist despite space and time. We are, down to every last one of our ancestors, no matter how far back we go, linked to the actions, thoughts, and emotions of each person with whom we share genetic material. You're a reincarnation, if you will, of every life that had to exist in order to make you. An echo of the lived lives of people, *all* the people, from your family tree.

Foster

"You'll never guess what happened," Foster sang, plopping down on my couch.

"What's up?"

"So, my grandma was in town last week and I was telling her about my new job."

And once again, my Spidey senses began to tingle.

Foster is twenty-eight and had come to me after her long-term relationship had ended abruptly—and not, rather heart-shatteringly, as a result of her own wishes. Any breakup can be hard, but it's made harder when a couple has spent much of their time doing activities that are the primary interest of only one partner, as had been the case in Foster's relationship. In those cases, the partner's world becomes your world, so a breakup means an end to not just your companionship but also your day-to-day life.

A few months prior to this moment, Foster had begun doing the work of identifying hobbies and interests of her own that she could devote her time to. Foster's parents had her when they were both in their teen years, and so she had spent much of her own adolescence parenting herself while her parents spent most of the time in their own process of growing up. When Foster left the chaos of her parents' house at eighteen, she threw herself into a string of monogamous, all-encompassing relationships with older men—anything she could do to find a stable "home." As a result, she never got the time to do any deep self-exploration.

During our work together, a fascination with being around

reptiles, specifically snakes, kept popping up. This seemingly random interest was intriguing for both of us. Foster hadn't been around reptiles as a youth, and there was no remembered exposure to them growing up. One day, as we completed another exploratory exercise in which reptiles came up, we both remembered that Foster often used the snake to represent herself during our very early sand tray sessions.[11]

The new job Foster is referring to is at a reptile center. She had begun working there a few weeks previous, in the serpentarium no less, learning how to care for and handle snakes. She took naturally to the reptiles and had even gotten a small snake tattoo, honoring her passion.

Back to today.

Foster goes on, enraptured. "She told me that my great-grandmother was legit a total snake person! She apparently had a whole room full and even had a snake tattoo! Can you imagine? At that time—a woman getting that kind of tattoo?"

She sat there, her mouth and eyes wide. Excitement emanating from her. "How could I not have known about this?! Man, I wish I could've met her."

Seeing the joy that came from her feeling a connection—an otherworldly connection to an ancestor she never even knew at that—was worth so much. Knowing there was so much more where that came from was a pretty close second.

---

[11] A sand tray is a therapeutic technique in which a client places figurines in sand to help express themselves without needing to use words.

7

The Eternal You

Do you not think that there are things which you cannot understand, and yet which are; that some people see things that others cannot? . . . Ah, it is the fault of our science that it wants to explain all; and if it explain not, then it says there is nothing to explain.

—BRAM STOKER, *DRACULA*

The concept of an Imprint isn't new. For instance, the idea that we pass some part of ourselves to others via progeny or otherwise has been part of religious and spiritual beliefs around the world even before written history began.[12] As the idea of writing slowly spread and those first communities were deciding what to record, they

----

[12] Writing has been around since roughly 3100 BCE but wasn't utilized in the same capacity it is today until over *four thousand* years later. For instance, printed books available for mass population consumption weren't available until 1439 CE. Thank you, printing press!

picked items that were deemed the most important. They chose laws, ideas, and stories, guidance that forever before had been transmitted orally—necessary wisdom passed on for each generation's lifetime.

In northern India, the term *reincarnation*—the passing on of one's life's essence into another human form—appeared in the Upanishads (the sacred scriptures of Hinduism) somewhere in the seventh or sixth centuries BCE. And around 580 BCE, we see the concept of reincarnation embraced by the Greek philosopher and mathematician Pythagoras. According to his contemporary, Xenophanes, Pythagoras tried to intervene on behalf of a beaten puppy, saying, "Stop, don't keep hitting him, since it is the soul of a man who is dear to me, which I recognized, when I heard it yelping." Moreover, the Bhagavad Gita, a Hindu text believed to have been written in the second or first centuries BCE, describes the idea of a life passing from one person to another: "Never did I not exist, nor you, nor these rulers of men; nor will any one of us ever hereafter cease to be. As, in this body, infancy and youth and old age (come) to the embodied (self), so does the acquisition of another body; a sensible man is not deceived about that" (Müller, 1882, p. 44).

In Kabbalah, a Jewish mysticism that's been around since at least the twelfth century, reincarnation is mentioned in both the Sefer HaBahir and the Shaar Hagilgulim. The Shaar Hagilgulim says, "There is not a generation which does not have someone like Avraham Avinu" (the founding father in the Bible) or one that doesn't contain someone like Moses (Afilalo, n.d.). Thus, each generation of humanity contains the same lives as the generations that have lived before. And in these texts, reincarnation isn't automatic. Rather, deciding to come back as another person is a choice that gets to be made by each soul. The purpose of reincarnation in the Kabbalah is much the same as in Buddhism. It's an attempt to reach the highest level of righteousness, which can be achieved by rectifying the failures that occurred in the life lived before. It's interesting to note that these failures could be anything from committing an act of violence to not marrying your soul mate.[13] And in the fifteenth century, the Yoruba people of West Africa finally documented the concept of reincarnation that they had been transmitting orally in their part of the world for centuries prior. In the Ifá corpus, the Yoruba sacred texts, it states that every person chooses a destiny before being reincarnated (Wilson, n.d.).

There's also "rebecoming," a cousin concept to reincarnation, which was a core teaching in Buddhism as early as the sixth century. Some Buddhist teachings discuss rebirth (which is more like reincarnation) occurring via a stream of consciousness, similar to the flame of a candle lighting another. In rebecoming, there is no permanent sense of self—no single flame; rather, each person is made up of energy (the same energy that Einstein mentioned does spooky things), which comes together to form a being (Bhikkhu, 2003). Upon death, those energies disperse into the ether, eventually to recombine with other energy to create a new, unique person.

Let us note, too, that it's not just through spiritual rebirth that the concept of transferring parts of the self to others occurs. For instance, there's a belief that eating a plant, especially one grown in the soil of something deceased, will transfer the energy of that deceased thing into you. And then there's cannibalism, which was fueled by the belief that eating a person's flesh or internal organs would endow the cannibal with some of the characteristics of the deceased. You might assume this is a belief that could only be held by Jeffrey Dahmer, but one of humanity's most widely respected visionaries echoed this sentiment. In his notebooks, Leonardo

---

[13] I should note that the text says only men can reincarnate, even though women's souls can still attach to another soul, which is totally patriarchal and speaks to the misogyny in religion, but that's commentary for another book entirely.

DaVinci stated, "We preserve our life with the death of others. In a dead thing insensate life remains which, when it is reunited with the stomachs of the living, regains sensitive and intellectual life."

In fact, for several hundred years on either side of the sixteenth and seventeenth centuries, Europeans from all walks of life, from scientists to royalty, routinely took medicine in which the most common ingredient was human body parts (Dolan, 2012). For the most part, it was powdered mummy parts, though "fresher" human meat was also encouraged. The thought was that the soul of a person was carried in the blood, the fresher the better, and by consuming parts of a corpse a person could gain some of the strength or characteristics of the person consumed.

And it wasn't just the Europeans during the Renaissance who took this idea to heart. Romans would drink the blood of dead gladiators because they thought doing so would allow them to absorb the vitality and strength of the deceased. And in other cultures and time periods, including ancient Mesopotamia and India, the usefulness of ingesting and utilizing human body parts as a way to take on part or all of the dead's qualities was a widely held belief. For instance, some cultures would eat the organs of captured enemies to gain memories, and thus useful information, from them. There are reports that assorted North American first peoples ate their enemies' hearts or other body parts in an effort to absorb some of the qualities of the deceased (Abler, 1980). Pekka Hämäläinen's (2019) *Lakota America: A New History of Indigenous Power* tells a story about the Iroquois people: "Whole villages joined in feasts where they consumed the corporal and spiritual power of their enemies" (p. 22). While the heart was eaten to gain courage and power, other parts of the body, such as the brain and tongue, were swallowed to assume knowledge and bravery.

And if you find that the idea that a person can gain virtues, skills, and memories by consuming another person reeks of pure superstition, I'd argue that's a bit of that black-and-white thinking I mentioned at the very beginning of our time together. Might I suggest instead looking into the grey, where even science suggests there may be some truth in the matter (as there always is). In 1960, psychologist James McConnell posited that memories exist outside of the brain and can be transferred between organisms. McConnell went on to train flatworms and then fed the bodies of those trained flatworms to other, untrained flatworms (McFarling and STAT, 2018). According to McConnell's findings, the untrained worms exhibited the behavior of the worms they'd cannibalized, suggesting that memories were somehow transferred.

McConnell's work became largely discredited—a bit because his work was hard to replicate at the time and a bit, I suspect, because people were just genuinely horrified and unsettled by his experiment. However, in 2013, scientists at Tufts University confirmed that McConnell really was onto something. In order to show that memories don't solely reside in the brain, Tal Shomrat and Michael Levin trained flatworms and then gave them a Marie Antoinette and cut off their heads. What they found was that when the flatworms' heads and brains regrew, they maintained the behaviors and memories they had held prior to their decapitation. Memories, the researchers surmised, truly are embedded in the whole body.

Another idea held within the Imprint—that the experiences of the past are like ghosts, motivating our behavior and ideas—is also echoed in ancient teachings. In many schools of Indian philosophy, the term *samskara* refers to psychological imprints that are left in the subconscious by our daily experiences. These imprints are not just passively shaping our actions and intentions but rather are active forces in our subconscious and conscious minds. Our samskaras constantly push us into action by influencing our thoughts, expectations, habits, and emotions. And since your actions in the now generate karma (a force that influences your next life), what you do now impacts all future versions of yourself. As the Dalai Lama said, "Imprints of past lives remain on the consciousness." In other words, your ancestors' rebirthed selves may actually be you, reliving the same life, trying this time to get it right.

There is so much in the core of ancient belief systems that echoes the concept of the Imprint. From our time together, we see that there's a sort of eternal life being created through epigenetics and the passing down of memories and experiences. We see that energy can never be lost and that what was once whole is forever entangled, and so life energy and memories can pass from one person to another instantly, a process that continues through birth, life, and death. And we see that, for as long as humans have existed, there has been a sense that the memories and experiences that occur in one human life can shape what occurs in another. No matter what angle we take, we keep coming back to the same place. And what that means for you, dear reader, is that there is a great deal of influence happening within and to you that you don't see.

**

Some people might be reading this book and internally screaming, "*But I'm not like either of my parents!*" But remember, as I've mentioned, the memories that get passed down go back generations, so the Imprint isn't only coming from your birth mother and father. Think of it like this: Your ancestral line is like a brand. And just like a brand, when hundreds or even thousands of years of life experiences are piled all together, there are just going to be some products that don't rise to the surface. Remember Crystal Pepsi? Yeah, no one does, and if you do, it's likely you don't remember much else about it except that it was clear and that it was gross. It was a blip that didn't survive in the memory of the generations of the Pepsi brand. And like that forgotten relic of a product, some of the traits of your mom or dad or grandmother or whoever might not make it into your Imprint.

But the core of your brand, crafted and honed over thousands of years, remains. There are thousands of droplets of water in a single cup of water. You don't taste each individual one, but they're there. If nothing in your parents' lives seems to resonate as you read through this book, go back a generation or two and you'll likely find a connection that does. You may be nothing like your mother and father but exactly like a grandparent, or even a great-great-grandparent.

I mean, imagine if someone took a copy of who you are *right now* and set it forth into the world. The copied version of you would have new experiences that would shape their decisions and life choices, but the same past that shapes you and your decisions would shape them as well. After all, people often behave in ways that echo their actions during similar situations in their own past (Albarracín and Wyer, 2000). And even if you think the actions of your past were dumb and you can't believe you were ever that stupid—if you had your own Crystal Pepsi moment—your past behavior still impacts your future decision making. Which means that unless you intentionally do something different, you *and* your copy would have similar reactions to conversations, situations, and chains of events, making the trajectory of your lives more similar than you might think. Likewise, whatever memories are in you, whatever Imprint is living in your cells, is an echo in a long, deep cavern, ever present but subtle, impacting your every move.

Katie

"I have never been a proper mother," Bonnie says to her now adult daughter, Katie. She has repeated this phrase multiple times today during our time together. This time she adds, "But I'm thankful that you're doing OK in spite of my many shortcomings."

"I wouldn't say I'm doing OK, but it has nothing to do with you," Katie responds sympathetically.

And I wish that were true, but it isn't. Katie is very much affected by what happened to her mother. But also, what happened to her mother's mother and father, and so on and so on. And we're here to uncover what that is. Bonnie and Katie, mother and daughter, are in a session track I've designed to dig deep into Katie's Imprint. This isn't about finding blame. It's about finding what hooks are pulling us this way and that. It's about seeing the energy that's already in motion, so that we can work to shift the trajectory of that energy into something more true to who we want to be.

Katie had originally asked me for help when she recognized that she was just constantly filled with anxiousness, agitation, and anger, sometimes all at once. We had been working through that until a few weeks ago, when Katie abruptly stated she was considering moving hundreds of miles away to start again. The move would put her in an area with no job, no support, and a full day's travel from her four-year-old daughter.

When I asked Katie why leaving seemed like the best solution, she stated, "It just . . . it feels like the right thing to do. I mean, it makes sense, you know? Like, I'm a mess. It will just be better if I'm out of her life."

"You don't think she's happy with you in her life now?" I questioned.

"Not really. I can't help her. She's got all this kid stuff going on and I'm supposed to be helping her grow up. But I can't even get my own life together," she asserted. And then, after a significant pause, she had added quietly, "How can I help her when I can't even help myself?"

Given that this decision would have such big consequences, I asked Katie if she would be interested in taking a few sessions to look at her Imprint prior to deciding. She agreed, and luckily we were able to have her mother, Bonnie, join us for a couple of the sessions.

Bonnie left Katie's father, Ken, when Katie was nine. According to Bonnie, Ken was extremely conservative and wanted a conservative household. He believed in corporal punishment, criticism as the best avenue for change, and traditional gender roles. He also expected Bonnie to serve as the primary caregiver for children, which resulted in Ken having very little interaction with Katie, the entirety of the parenting falling on Bonnie. In addition, Ken felt he should be the sole breadwinner, refusing to let Bonnie be employed, and he traveled extensively for his job, often being away for weeks at a time, leaving Bonnie feeling alone, lonely, and overwhelmed.

Bonnie had grown up in a conservative household, so when she first met Ken, his worldview felt like a comfort. But as the years and eventual tears went on, she found herself rebelling against his approach. As such, Bonnie and Ken's relationship became strained and eventually just felt like too much for Bonnie to endure. Katie and her mother had been inseparable since Katie was born, but as the situation for herself became insufferable, Bonnie saw no other way out but to leave.

"He said he wasn't going anywhere. He said that if I was un-happy, I would have to go," Bonnie remembered sadly. "I either had to stay in what I would describe as an abusive relationship, or leave. And so I left."

Since Bonnie didn't yet have a job or a stable home, Ken got primary custody of Katie. In this abruptly changed environment, Katie struggled to find a sense of home with her father—thrust into an existence that suddenly felt foreign. Adding to Katie's despair, Bonnie relocated to another town after the divorce, and due to the distance and Bonnie's need to work odd jobs to make ends meet, Katie and Bonnie saw less and less of each other until contact was reduced to intermittent. Sincere attempts had been made to stay connected, but over time, visits became a rarity.

Distraught and slowly robbed of her ability to turn to her mother—her comfort—for help, Katie's life became a nightmare. We all have a fight/flight/freeze response that gets triggered when we're scared, and Katie's default mode was fight. And boy, did she fight everything. The relationship between Katie and her father deterio-rated quickly, the pair engaged in constant battle. And as soon as her diploma was in hand, Katie left Ken's house, never to return.

Physically alone for the first time, Katie did what many others do when faced with an oppressive nightly silence and their own thoughts. She scrambled to find a relationship—any relationship—that could make her feel comforted, even for just a moment. She had spent years desperate to feel connected, and flirtation made her feel nice after years of feeling nothing but anger and distress. But her anger was at the helm, and her attraction was to explosions and fire. A still lake is no match for a tidal wave, and so Katie found partners who would clash and fight too.

She spent the next decade leaping in and out of unhealthy re-lationships in a vacillating state of anger and loneliness. She moved often, in a constant escape, an avoidance of feelings she couldn't soothe no matter how hard she tried. And then she met David.

David had been a friend first, then had decided to throw his affections Katie's way. She admitted she didn't want to be with him initially, but then loneliness took over and she eventually agreed to date him in order to fill the space still haunting her. David was even-tempered, which was a complete shift from Katie's long string of highly emotional relationships, and so when David asked Katie to marry him, she accepted, assuming that his even temper was a good sign.

But David and Katie's life together proved volatile nevertheless, and their relationship was consistently unstable. Katie had never processed the trauma of her childhood, and so her anger and anxiousness continued, clashing instead of melding with David's seemingly even temper. David, in turn, became increasingly critical of Katie, failing to see why his behavior didn't change hers—or rather, why she couldn't just be like him. David eventually drew his parents into the criticisms, leaving Katie constantly feeling under attack.

In time, Katie became pregnant. As would be expected, the pregnancy did little to quell Katie's anxiety and she became transfixed with the idea she was going to be a terrible mother. Fueling that fear, the criticisms from David appeared to increase, with the new fodder of questioning Katie's ability to mother. In addition, David had to travel a lot for work, so Katie spent a large portion of her pregnancy either alone or having to rely on David's parents, who were by now outwardly judgmental toward her. In addition, the pregnancy was difficult for Katie, and she suffered migraines, swollen joints, and preeclampsia.

Katie's anxiety spiraled, she felt alone, and these conditions along with the fear of being a failure as a mother became a debilitating trifecta as she felt she failed to successfully navigate the landscape of pregnancy. This trend continued after Katie gave birth, and she found both David and his parents in constant combat with her on how she mothered. Suffering constantly from feelings of loneliness, incompetence, and ultimately unlovability, she filed for divorce. Just over a year later, Katie expressed her desire to make the aforementioned change and leave her life and child behind.

In every large decision a person makes, it's important to look at the Imprint. We need to understand not only what might be contributing to the feelings a person is having but also what might be contributing to a person's thinking. A mother voluntarily moving far away from her children because of marital dissatisfaction feels very big. Before deciding how to move forward, then, we needed to dig deep. How was Katie reconciling this choice? Were her feelings only stemming from the intense marital dissatisfaction or was there more? Was it possible that because her mother had left her, it made it easier for Katie to leave?

When I spoke with Bonnie, I asked lots of probing questions. I asked about environment. About temperament. I asked about things mother and daughter had never spoken of. And once I was done, the gut feeling that there was something more than someone's own life experiences could account for was confirmed. To ignore the impact of the Imprint would have been to ignore a piece of Katie's puzzle. To ignore the Imprint would lead to disastrous results.

"I was alone when I was pregnant with her," Bonnie told me. "Ken was in Europe on business and couldn't be with me."

David was away on travel through much of Katie's pregnancy.

"I had no job. I was staying with my mom and dad, so I didn't have a place of my own. I was anxious. Lonely. Sad. I was . . ." Bonnie paused for a moment. "I was *scared*. Katie was my first child. I didn't know what to expect."

Anxiety. Sadness. Fear. Loneliness. All experienced by Katie too.

"You did fine, Mom," Katie interjected, her need to comfort her mother a sign of the words she herself needed to hear.

"Were you worried about being a good mother?" I asked.

"I was! I felt totally lost. How would I manage? Would I have help?"

"What about your husband?" I inquired.

Bonnie responded sheepishly. "Ken . . . wasn't sure about our marriage at the time. He also wanted a boy, not a girl. I wasn't sure he would be accepting of Katie when she came. It was an unstable marriage. And I had to deal with both sets of parents telling me how to do this or that."

Katie felt constantly criticized by David's parents as well.

"You weren't confident in yourself as a parent?" I inquired.

"Back then, I lacked confidence and was still trying to discover who 'me' was. I wasn't sure of anything!" Bonnie stated. Then she added, "And in the end, that's why I ended up leaving."

At that, Katie took notice.

"I thought you left because you and Dad . . ." Katie started.

"Well, that was part of it," Bonnie confirmed. "But more so, it was more because I just . . . I knew I wasn't a good mom."

Katie stared, the feeling hitting too close to home.

"I started to think it was better if I stayed out of her life," Bonnie told me, remorsefully. "I was a mess. How could I help her when I couldn't even help myself?"

And there it was. The echo of Katie's very own words, her own thoughts, said aloud by her mother. Feelings Bonnie had experienced decades prior in an almost identical situation. A cycle reliving itself.

***

It's not hard to imagine that a child who loses a mother's presence and gets stuck in a volatile, seemingly unloving relationship with her father would then turn to unhealthy relationships capped by poor coping skills and choices. Earlier in my career, I would have focused only on that trauma. We would work on reparenting the self from that hurt place. On understanding unconditional love, for others and the self. But now, as I have come to understand what hidden influences often lie within the Imprint, it means there's more that needs to be done.

Healing childhood trauma doesn't fully free us from the negative impacts of our past. And it wasn't going to keep Katie from making a decision she would most certainly grow to regret. Katie is, in many ways, reliving her mother's life. A mother, fearful and anxiety-ridden, feeling unloved and incompetent, bears a child. That same mother finds she longs to escape her stressors but can't figure out how, and in an act of desperation she flees, leaving her child. The child grows up to be fearful and anxiety-ridden, feeling unloved and incompetent, and also bears a child. And that child, now an adult, finds she also longs to escape her stressors but can't figure out how, and in an act of desperation wants to flee, leaving her child.

Truth be told, it's hard to accept that Katie didn't see the similarities between her mother and her before we did work on the Imprint. I mean, as we read it here, it's hard to ignore. But the brain and body do amazing things to keep us moving. When you're in it, all you see is what's in front of you. We rarely stop to analyze what's happening.

8

The Rippling Pond

In the Ramtop village where they dance the real Morris dance, for example, they believe that no one is finally dead until the ripples they cause in the world die away—until the clock he wound up winds down, until the wine she made has finished its ferment, until the crop they planted is harvested. The span of someone's life, they say, is only the core of their actual existence.

—TERRY PRATCHETT, *REAPER MAN*

The momentum behind your life was a ball in motion before you were born. You are, after all, a sort of reincarnation of your parents, and of the ancestral lives that created them, too. You are you, of course. But you are also very much them. Their existence becoming a wave, pushing out, onward, forever into the infinite. A ripple of energy that started with your first ancestors, continuing its journey through the universe's eternal pond. You weren't born still, a bowling ball sitting in the cradle, waiting to be picked up.

Instead, you came into creation with the ball already in motion, already rushing down the lane, following the trajectory laid out by the arm swing of many people long before you.

Remember the twin brothers Jack and Oskar, who were split between their birth parents? In an interview, Jack, the twin who lived with his biological father, said, "I always thought that I picked up my nervous habits, like fidgeting with other people's rubber bands and paper clips from my father." But instead of it being a learned behavior, it turned out it was something *in* him. "[Oskar's] the same way," Jack noted, realizing his behavior was not learned (Grimes, 2015). The brothers both got those specific traits because they *are*, in some ways, their father.

I once met with a single father who was diagnosed with a genetic medical issue. The condition, which he had since birth, is potentially fatal, and he had come to me to help process medical anxiety he struggled with as a result. His daughter was young—seven years old—and he had chosen to keep his diagnosis private, never discussing doctors' visits or symptoms with her out of fear that she would begin to worry about her own health. But one day he lamented that his daughter had started to show signs of medical anxiety despite having no medical issues. She was asking questions, obsessed with specific ailments that oddly included the same symptoms as his illness. And what's more, she'd started talking about her fears of death in ways that echoed what he had been saying in sessions, seemingly tapping into the private thoughts he had been having.

I've talked with a grandmother who complained that she tried to make different choices while raising her grandson in her daughter's absence, but he turned out "just like his mother despite it all." I worked with a man who found out late in life that his career was the exact same one his father had chosen. Which wouldn't typically be remarkable except that for decades he thought another man was his father, and the man only came to know he had a different birth father when he was already an adult, his career well under way.

It's a kind of recycling, the retelling of a story over and over again in the tomes of our lives. And what's more, everyone is there with you. After all, all of our trajectories started in the same places. Human existence is forever unfolding, the first of our species a tightly packed square, fanning out as the millennia went on. Our collective pool of ancestors starting small and growing larger. So perhaps, because our trajectories all come from the same few sources, we're all out here living similar lives. And not just similar lives to our ancestors, but similar to one another. Over and over, time and time again.

There's been a viral running joke recently that all men think about the Roman Empire at least once a week. And I found myself wondering, is it just a relic of history class or is there something more to it? Why don't women report this obsession? Could it be a collective echo—Roman ancestors repeating the thoughts to all European-descended men of today?[14] Lives reliving lives reliving lives. Perhaps that's why we keep repeating the mistakes of past generations. Perhaps *that's* why history repeats itself. Perhaps that's why society always seems to find itself on the same damn path.

---

[14] It's typically only those of European descent who reported thinking about the Roman Empire, and now I totally want to see if there exists a sort of collective descendant rumination upon ancestral groups. Someone get me some funding!

9

Your Open Door

The most beautiful thing we can experience is the mysterious. It is the source of all true art and science. He to whom the emotion is a stranger, who can no longer pause to wonder and stand wrapped in awe, is as good as dead; his eyes are closed.

—ALBERT EINSTEIN

Science, for all its strengths, is a system built on reductionism and isolation. It focuses on separation, on trying to distill out single elements. But nothing in our world is singular. Everything from plants to people are in actuality complex systems. Everything is in a relationship with something else, and science does not and cannot know all the elements that impact any particular thing.

Take for instance an herb used for healing, St. John's wort.

Science has tried to study the herb by testing singular components of the plant to determine whether St. John's wort actually "works." But these studies don't account for the myriad relationships that can impact the efficacy of the results, such as the source of the herb that they use in the study. Could wild St. John's wort function differently than one grown for medical study? Do the scientists really know what impact the weather conditions the months prior to harvesting may have had on the herb itself? Would a person who ate a diet rich in vitamins have a better outcome from using the herb than someone whose diet consisted of processed foods? Despite efforts to control variables, science simply cannot account for everything, thus impacting what research studies can and cannot tell us.

Science, for all its strengths, is also very rigid. And this rigidity can prevent it from exploring things outside of what is currently *en vogue*. Ecologist Christina Richards, a scientist attempting to look at epigenetics to see how much it might affect human evolution, speaks to this bias. Zimmer (2022), writing in *The Scientist*, notes that Richards believes "with DNA-based changes dominating evolutionary theory for so long, it may well be an uphill battle to convince scientists that other mechanisms contribute. 'We've been steered by that opinion for a long time,' [Richards] says. 'If you define evolution as changing allele frequency over time, then we have nowhere to start, and that's the real problem. . . . I'm not trying to say that it's all epigenetic. I'm just trying to ask the question [whether it's involved].'"

And if we're being honest, to assume that science can give us all the answers is to once again dismiss what women, minorities, and centuries of indigenous healers have known and practiced. Trying to control the version of what is "true" via a field that has historically been run primarily by white, European males is to remove the experiences of a plethora of people. Sadly, the field of mental health is no better. My field dictates what is *taught* to be true rather than what is *experienced* to be so. It strong-arms compliance to only use "evidenced-based" practices, which in no uncertain terms dismisses a great deal of what is helpful. What's more, it gatekeeps growth by using expensive education and certification programs—ask any community mental health person how many continuing education credits they need to keep their license and get ready for a rant. Even worse, it takes indigenous healing practices and repackages them as its own. Just look at the concept of "mindfulness," which is a practice that's been utilized by many cultures well before mainstream psychotherapy decided to (re)coin it and make money off of it.

Try as it might, science cannot always prove what a person knows and feels in the depths of their being. Outside of what we think we know is a vast world of things we don't, and betwixt the two is a bottomless pit of misunderstandings and partial knowledge. This is where subjects like metaphysics, mysticism, faith, ethereality, and even multiverses have the space to exist. And it is in the realms of subjects we don't and likely can't fully comprehend that there likely are numerous other doorways through which we might be Imprinted.

Take for instance microchimerism, which is the cells of one individual appearing in another (Shrivastava et al., 2019). It most often occurs during pregnancy, when a mother-to-be gives some of her cells to her developing fetus via the placenta. This giving of cells is also bidirectional, which means a mother's baby gives some of its cells to her in return. So a mother of a child could have not one but two sets of microchimeric cells in her body—one set from her child and the other from her own mother. A scientist studying these types of cells estimated that "one out of a million cells in our body is not our own" (Mackenzie, 2023). With roughly thirty-six trillion cells in a human body, and given what we've already discussed about DNA within each cell and about spooky action, that's quite a lot of memories grabbing chairs at your dinner table.

And then there's the potential Imprint from mitochondrial DNA. Mitochondria are located in the fluid of each cell's nucleus, and their job is to convert the energy from the food you eat into something your cells can use. Most of the DNA in your body—referred to as your nuclear DNA—is from both sets of parents. But mitochondrial DNA is exclusively maternal, which means you inherited it from your mother, who inherited it from her mother, and so on. And unlike your nuclear DNA, which breaks down quickly and is unique to each individual, mitochondrial DNA is a direct pass from a mother to her offspring (Merheb et al., 2019). Scientists use this type of DNA to trace information back, person by person, throughout your entire maternal history, to your family's metaphoric Eve.

All of a female baby's egg cells are created while she is growing inside her mother's womb, at roughly the fourth month of gestation. This means that when your birth mother was in your grandmother's uterus, half of *you* already existed. The DNA you got from your mother—tucked in the egg that created you—was coded with memory when your mother was not yet even born. And because your DNA, already packed away in the egg cell of your yet-to-be-born mother, lived inside your grandmother for roughly five months, both your birth mother's and your grandmother's lives—their experiences, thoughts, and feelings—*directly* influenced who you would become (Kirshenbaum, 2023). Taking it further, your grandmother's DNA was inside both her mother and her own grandmother (your great-great-grandmother), and you can keep doing that back through the roughly four thousand or so ancestors you have had to have for you to be alive today. The origin and subsequent evolution of your *entire* maternal family line is in every cell of your body.

So call it what you want. Nature and nurture. Epigenetics. Quantum action. Reincarnation. Your family's metaphoric Eve. In the end, they all lead to the same end: influence and Imprint. The truly eternal retention of the memories of a life. All any memory needs is an open door.

* * *

Everything that needs to be said has already been said. But since nobody listens we have to keep going back and beginning all over again.

-ANDRÉ GIDE

My work is about helping people live intentional lives. I focus on systemic reconstruction, not just symptom reduction. Systemic changes, the ones that are led from inside you, are more sustainable forms of well-being. And there is so very much a person can do to achieve true, soul-inspired change even with the Imprint. Even if you're skeptical of every single bit of this book, taking responsibility for yourself and future generations isn't really something that should be up for debate. Even if you don't want to see the grey, take owning your own existence as your starting point and let's go from there. We are, after all, living on this planet together. I want you to be happier because it helps all of us. And I want you to be happier by becoming, well, you.

As Jean-Jacques Rousseau wrote in *The Social Contract* (1762), "As soon as any man says of the affairs of the State 'What does it matter to me?' the State may be given up for lost." It would be supremely naive and egotistical to assume that our actions only affect our inner sphere and that we hold no responsibility for those outside of our direct influence. And maybe, just maybe, I wrote this book in hope. That even if my theory of the Imprint has holes, it still inspires people to do more. To look deeper. To try to stop the mindless progression of bad behavior. Hope for our species to be something more than a drain upon this earth and one another.

Looking around today, it's hard to have hope that the masses of people who inhabit this world have forethought for their own future, let alone the future of later generations. But if you truly live on forever, a part of you passed on and living in someone else, would you make different choices? If what you pass down isn't just what's written in a will but also the memories and experiences you've gained, would you change your life to avoid the negative consequences of a life that's already been lived? Even if you don't plan to have children, we've seen that stress and trauma can create epigenetic changes that can impact you now, here, in this life, increasing your risk for all kinds of problems, including mood and anxiety issues (Klengel and Binder, 2015). Would you change your behavior to rid yourself of the burdens of the generations who lived before? Change to be free to live a truly unique life? Maybe if we all did, then we could, as Nelson Henderson reportedly advised, plant trees under whose shade we will never sit. Maybe then, we could gift the world, and possibly future generations, something besides the same lives that have been lived before.

I hope.

10

Phantoms

We lie best when we lie to ourselves.

—STEPHEN KING, *IT*

Ultimately, the Imprint questions one of the most prolific dogmas in Western society today—the idea that you are fully in charge of your own life. In fairness, it's not easy for many people to accept that what someone does in the years before they have children has an impact on the fate of those same children. And once you throw in the added possibility that we can hold memories from our grandparents, or even our grandparent's parents? That's a hard pill to swallow for many. To accept it changes *everything*.

How do you know the passion you're pursuing is really yours and not a holdover from one of your ancestors? An unmet dream passed on for you to complete? Does the disruptive anger you're feeling over a particular situation come from you or from a generations-old wound? Are you truly choosing your own vacation spot, or is there some memory from a generation ago pushing you there? Do you take that stressful job, knowing your child might be born with anxiety because of it? Would you still enlist in the military if you knew that as a result your own children might die earlier than they would have otherwise? What decisions are you making now that could potentially reduce your offspring's ability to survive? How about your own?

Every environment you put yourself in—*every* decision you make—is suspect once you start investigating the Imprint. And what's more, it's a wake-up call that your own experiences could pass into your bloodline for *generations*. It brings a whole new perspective to Shakespeare's *Merchant of Venice* quote "The sins of the father are to be laid upon the children." To see that quote through the lens of the Imprint? That's some heavy shit. Because it means preventing retribution against your family isn't the only concern you should have. It means you need to be cautious of your behavior because the life you live becomes, quite literally, Imprinted onto your children, an eternal echo of you that lasts seemingly forever. An Imprint that, to some extent, dictates the future lives of your children and of all subsequent generations of your line.

There's already a plethora of evidence on the negative outcomes our offspring can suffer, based on our individual choices, that has nothing to do with the Imprint. The scientific literature is stuffed with the many ways stress, nutrition, lifestyle, and countless other things can impact both a developing fetus and a reared child. And it's not just the overt "Yeah, we know it's bad" stuff, like drug and alcohol use. For instance, did you know that mothers who take acetaminophen during pregnancy can risk their daughters developing early puberty or their sons having low testosterone? Or that general acetaminophen use is associated with an increase in attention deficit/hyperactivity disorder (ADHD) diagnosis in offspring (Bauer et al., 2021)? You even have to be careful *when* you choose to get pregnant. A study published in 2006 showed that men born in a year when there were fewer men than women lived longer than men born when the ratio of men to women was high (Paul, 2010, p. 129).

But despite all that we know, the notion that a parent's choices have *such* a significant influence on how a child behaves was and is a conceptual land mine. And as I mentioned way back in the beginning of this book, when we start to look to parents as an explanation for the behaviors and other troubles of children, we get into some very risky territory. For instance, one study found that mothers of autistic children reported feeling frequently insulted or humiliated by others because of their child's behavior and diagnosis, and consequently they had more than a 20% higher risk of suicidality (Jahan et al., 2020). When we start to look at how parents are impacting their children, we too often end up running into a blame game. It raises the same question that comes up after every murder. Every school shooting. Every act of antisocial behavior.

Where does the impact of inherited traits end and self-determination begin?

Just posing the question has ramifications, let alone debating an answer to it. And as we've already discussed, when we turn a collective gaze to trying to craft children with more "desirable" traits, we step way too quickly into the very likely chance that someone will start touting eugenics. Someone will inevitably believe that by selective breeding or getting rid of certain people/traits, we can have a better society.

We're back to that black-and-white thinking again. What kind of tragedy would we see if every ailment, every non–socially acceptable behavior, was blamed on parents? And if we start focusing on how a parent's decisions impact offspring, could we be promoting a misleading narrative of hopelessness? Are we able to aptly sort through that can of worms? The very real risks in these thoughts have frightened most people away from looking too deeply into what we inherit from our biological families.

And I have to admit we're probably not ready to truly tackle this question as a society. We're not capable of digging into the importance of parental choices without subsequently vilifying the parent or becoming too set on removing self-responsibility. And let's be honest, history has shown that most of the blame would fall on the female parent. We've been blaming women for societal woes since Adam and Eve. We're just too black-and-white in our collective thinking—we have lost the realization that we live in the grey.

In fairness, society as a whole hasn't completely gone off the rails, blaming and not helping, with what we currently know. Not yet anyway. With regard to a newborn, there is some small attempt to optimize maternal physical health. And in even more fairness, many other industrialized countries are well ahead of the United States on this particular matter. Things like maternity and paternity leave, adequate and affordable child care, and access to health care services are definitely a step in the right direction. But there is still so little done to help maternal *mental* health, let alone the physical and mental health of the father, that I find myself wondering what progress we're actually making.

For instance, society focuses quite a bit on a woman's use of alcohol during pregnancy, but did you know that a father's alcohol consumption *before* pregnancy could lead to issues? In an article published in the *Journal of Clinical Investigation*, Kara Thomas and colleagues (2023) found that male alcohol consumption before conception could also lead to fetal alcohol syndrome, and further, could lead to facial growth defects. Society also talks about reducing stress as a way to ensure healthy offspring. "It's not good for the baby," people say passively, almost routinely. But what are we *actually* doing as a society to help pregnant women live their best lives? What are we *actually* doing to ensure that a father-to-be is mentally and physically in a healthy place in the days, months, and even years prior to passing on his genetic makeup? But again, I suspect we're collectively a bit too selfish for that. In the United States, we can't even give people access to health care or food without the question of whether they "deserve" it.

No. If we were ready, if society were truly open to seeing what is actually woven into the tapestry of our being, we would ensure that people—*all* people—could succeed, knowing that to do so is to help humanity by improving each generation. We would treat everyone like they're holding the keys to the fucking universe. Because if the parents' environment is so important, if we're handing memories and traumas and influences down through generations—hell, if our cells are spookily tied to our loved ones through time and space? Well, then we absolutely are holding the keys to the universe. Each one of us. The mental health and well-being of any single person is paramount, and it will impact the entirety of humanity for eternity.

* * *

Your past is your shadow. It has form but no substance,
except in the places you allow it to touch you.
—TANANARIVE DUE, *BLOOD COLONY*

So why did I write this book if I don't think we're ready to ask
these questions? Because though we may not be ready collectively
to have these deep conversations, I do think we can individually. As
Agent K says in *Men in Black*, "People are dumb, panicky dangerous
animals." But the individual person? They're smart. They're capable.
You, dear reader, are capable. And if you've made it this far, it's
time. Time to rid yourself of the ghosts of ancestors who didn't
know better. Time to become a healthier you, so we can become a
healthier society. It's clear that the snowball effect is in play here.
The more times a specific trait gets passed down to the next generation without anyone trying to fix it, the greater is the probability
that it will become ingrained, harder and harder to heal in future
generations. And even for those who won't be passing on pieces
of themselves to biological offspring, the impact your ancestors are
having on your life can't be denied. And if you're not careful, you'll
spend your entire lives fighting someone else's fight. Living someone
else's dream. Perpetually discontented but unsure why.

Most people that start out on the journey I'm proposing end up
fighting with themselves for a while just trying to figure it all out.
Comfort in the "what is" is an extremely powerful force. It's the
devil you know. Being stuck where you are is only as painful as we
let it be, and it's sometimes easier to be stuck in a house that's falling
apart than to burn it all down on nothing but a hope that you can
build a better one. Staring at ashes is a really, really tough sell.

Burning it all down to see what remains, what is truly you and not remnants of someone else, may feel like a unpalatable task. But if you don't try, if you never dare to see life with an unhaunted mind, how can you ever know what life could truly be?

Martin

"I just don't think I can do this."

Martin is a thirty-eight-year-old father of three. He came to me because he needed surgery but couldn't bring himself to go through with it. Medical anxiety crippled his ability to do what needed to be done. Very early on in our work together, we were able to pinpoint a spawn event for that particular worry, linking the start of this anxiety to a fear-invoking incident that occurred when Martin was a teen. Thus, over the course of several months, we were able to break down the anxiety into manageable chunks and Martin had been able to schedule his surgery and attend all preliminary appointments. In parallel to this progress, Martin and I also realized that medical anxiety was a trait of almost everyone in his family. But now, with the rescheduled date of the new procedure just a week away, Martin found himself once again crippled by anxiety about what was to come.

"What's the story that you keep telling yourself about going through with it?" I asked.

"It's not really a story," Martin replied. "It's more like just sheer panic. I just jump right to 'I'm going to die on that table.'"

It was then that I suspected there was something more to Martin's anxiety. Words and feelings were coming from somewhere else, completely out of Martin's control, completely disassociated from his own experiences. I knew then that in order to overcome this challenge, we had to tackle his Imprint.

I sent Martin home that day with a task to dig into his family medical history. Not simply the anxieties, but the outcomes. What had happened to others? What other experiences existed that might be influencing him?

Three days later, Martin sent me a note. His great-grandfather had needed emergency surgery following an injury during war. While on the table, the great-grandfather coded, dying for forty-five seconds before the medical team was able to resuscitate him and bring him back.

With this knowledge, Martin was able to make his surgery date. In knowing its source, Martin was able to distance himself from the pervasive thought that had been impacting his behavior. The thought wasn't his, and so he treated it as such—the words of a concerned relative that just didn't know any better.

These seemingly rogue sentiments—the fear of an outcome that doesn't seem to have any justification—are not unusual for the Imprint. We can work through all the things that happened in our lives until the cows come home, but if the Imprint is still there, we might not be able to shake persistent feelings that impact our behavior, no matter how much progress we make on ourselves. In order to truly cleanse our house, we have to uncover all our ghosts.

11

An Exorcism

One is never afraid of the unknown; one is afraid of
the known coming to an end.

—KRISHNAMURTI

As I said in the beginning, this book lives in the grey. The Imprint isn't nature or nurture—it's both, and neither. And to be clear,
it's not a sure thing you have an Imprint from every single ancestor.
Just from a DNA perspective, according to the genomics company
23andMe, there's a 5% chance you inherit absolutely no DNA from
a fifth great-grandparent. Eventually, once you get out far enough,
you might be able to skip worrying about the Imprinted influence
of a person or two (Esselmann, 2020).

But what's more, the Imprint's influence isn't finite, genetics be
damned. Just because you inherited something doesn't mean you're
stuck with it. Your DNA changes as you age, possibly more than
20% over a decade, never mind all the ways you can intentionally
modify your behaviors to have a different outcome (Bjornsson et al.,

2008). You *can* close some of those ancestral doors. Further more, if you can figure out how to live a life of your own choosing, you could even reverse some of the traumas that have been passed down through the Imprint.

In 2016, Isabelle Mansuy—the mice researcher noted previously—wanted to see if some of the traumatized mice could be saved from passing down all of the problematic changes by placing them in a safe, healthy environment (Gapp et al., 2016). And lo and behold, traumatized mice raised in an enriched, healthy environment did *not* pass all of the genetic trash heap onto their pups. The genetics passed down from the mice raised in healthy environments differed from the genetics passed down by their brothers and sisters raised in the same traumatic environments. Living a mentally healthy life changed the mice at their core, and in a single generation changed the outcomes of the generation that came next.

Much like demonic possession, The Imprint can be very powerful in making us do some crazy shit, but it is not an all-powerful influence. The priests were still able to sequester Regan to her bed, after all.[15] Ancestral memories may put thoughts in our head and desires in our heart, but these in and of themselves don't move us to act. Yes, there are messages whispered to us from forefathers and -mothers, trying to persuade us even when we're not paying attention. But they're just that—whispers. They're suggestions, not puppet strings. Outside of breathing, pumping blood, and the other survivalesque actions your body has, every other action is a choice.

Even if we can't rid ourselves of the Imprint, we can see these whispers for what they are. And by doing so, we can become less influenced by them. As the Dalai Lama ("Reincarnation") states, we can be "cleared of all destructive emotions, as well as their imprints,"

---

[15] If you don't know this reference, you're missing a core part of any good horror fan's knowledge. Go see *The Exorcist* before you do anything else this week.

if we gain wisdom and enlighten the mind. And so we *must* focus on learning about ourselves—about the things that are influencing us. We must focus on recognizing and reducing the blind acquiescence to our own Imprints so that we can form unique, healthier, and truer lives.

Most people would support the idea that there is power and strength behind intentional living, and I think we all kind of know, deep down, that learning and working on the self can radically alter the impact we have on the world. If you can stop yourself from living out dead dreams and actions, if you can stop the ball from slogging on forever forward, you can move yourself into whatever else there might be out there in the chasm of existence, energy, and matter.

Many of us go through life never questioning the direction we're headed. We charge forth, convinced that whatever path we're on was one of our own choosing. But if you put effort into dissecting the map, into looking at what hidden influences might drive your actions, you're able to find something truly exceptional. You can, quite literally, change your stars. You can forge something completely and utterly new. And with that, I have one more story to tell.

My own.

Crystal

It was a rainy Thanksgiving morning and I was the saddest I'd ever been, which for a girl who ran away from home when she was a teen is saying a lot. My family might claim (or would have claimed at the time) that I was rather prone to melancholy, and in fairness to them, it is a state of being I was supremely comfortable being in. But on that rainy morning, I felt beyond melancholy. I felt broken. And not just, like, disappointed or bummed. Full-on heart-feels-like-it's-seizing, throat-tight, wake-up-filled-with-dread broken.

My mother used to tell me this story. I was three years old and she had taken me to a party, where I immediately caught the eye of a gentleman who swooped me up and fawned over me for quite some time. Apparently I was rather smitten with the attention, so much so that when his girlfriend came over and he attempted to hand me back to my mother, I was inconsolable. My mom said I wouldn't stop crying, no matter what she attempted, and would only calm if he brought his attention back to me.

At that early age, I was already in love with "love."[16] As years passed, my desire to feel loved was front and center of my being. I was never a romantic in the passive sense. I had no patience for being wooed, no stomach for the waiting that came with anticipation. Instead, I sought out love aggressively and with purpose. I desired the state of adoration consistently, and sadly, this took its toll.

---

[16] I put *love* in quotes here because what I understood to be love as a child was in fact not love but rather the mask of love. Obviously I didn't know that then, or until I was quite a bit older, but given that so much of my work involves helping people properly identify what love is and is not, I thought it important to distinguish between the two.

Throughout my adolescence and early adulthood, I endured a string of utterly terrible relationships, all in the name of seeking love. I was forever saddled with a person who was themself a volcano, the peace always disrupted by unhealthiness. Passion entangled in fear can look a lot like love to someone who doesn't know any better.

The outcome of all this chaos was a vast résumé of all makes and models of horrendous behavior. I've been cheated on and done the cheating, and I've been abused both emotionally and, to some extent, though it's embarrassing to admit, physically. I felt everything so strongly and I hurt too much all the time. And yet I couldn't let go of the notion that this was my reason for life—to find love. And so it went on for decades. The constant jump from crappy relationship to crappy relationship. Slowly shattering whatever slivers of my spirit remained.

And on that Thanksgiving back in 2013, I was still there. Still desperately seeking this thing I thought was my mission to find. Ironically, I was married at the time. But as with all the others, my relationship felt hollow. And what's more, my entire *life* felt wrong. I would look at it and get the sense I was living in somebody else's desires. The Talking Heads' line "How did I get here?" felt like it was written just for me.[17]

So there I was, running while dispirited. I had started to run for exercise because it got me out of the house and was, frankly, the only time I could focus on my thoughts. There's something about running that forces my thoughts to not come all at once. Plus, for me—a bit of a marshmallow by nature—any physical exertion requires a great deal of my attention to ensure I don't end up splayed on the pavement in a case of miscued coordination. And

---

[17] If you don't know that song ("Once in a Lifetime") or that band, do yourself a favor and pause here go listen to it. And when you're finished listening to that, go on to "Rock Lobster." That song...it's divine.

because my brain was spending all its resources ensuring I didn't go skidding across the asphalt, the other thoughts in my head were forced to line up in succession—a caravan having to single file it through a tight mountain pass. And it was then that my puzzle pieces gathered to show me a story I could finally see.

I had spent all my life trying to feel loved. The directive had been etched on my soul seemingly before I was born, and I had spent my entire life on a journey that had led me to nothing but despair. And to be fair, I hadn't really been taught healthy ways to love. I would be remiss to not acknowledge that played its part in my mess of a life. My childhood was filled with the trickle-down effects of trauma.

Don't get me wrong. My parents loved me. And both my mother and father are good people in the depths of themselves. I'm pretty sure the only person who has a more tender heart than I do is my mother. But both my parents had trauma as kids. They both had their struggles. So what they could give my sister and I was stunted. It was the best they could do at the time, not for lack of trying. But the one thing we just couldn't get quite right as a family was the sense of safety that comes from unconditional love. Not physical safety, but safety in the sense that you know in your bones there is someone there who has your back no matter what. That you are never alone. That no matter what, you will be OK. The ease, the peace, of knowing you have someone who will catch you if you fall didn't exist for my parents, so how on earth could they model it for their children?

This lack of modeling most surely impacted the types of relationships I chose. It's also where traditional therapeutic work usually stops—at a recognition of that type of impact. And there are many people who will claim success after achieving this recognition. But there is more to my story—to all our stories. Even if I had healthy role models, would I have been satiated? Would anything ever be enough? What *was* enough? I couldn't even answer that. Yet the tale that this—this idea of finding love—was my purpose in life? This tale lived within me for as long as I could remember. What would happen, I finally pondered, if I gave it all up? If I stopped running that race. What would happen if I rejected the story of a life I had always thought was mine?

I remember that the idea surprised me. I had written poems and ponderings and self-identified as a person in love with love for as long as I could write and remember. Actively choosing to not seek it out—to not follow that path—felt like a betrayal to myself. *You're just giving up!* something inside my head yelled at me. But it was too late. I had gone through a door, and I looked at that statement not as fact but with curiosity—with analysis.

It's not giving up. I told myself. *I'm choosing to focus on something else for once, and if I never find love, so be it.* So I went home after my run and told my now ex-husband I wanted a different life. One that was about existing in a space that didn't make me miserable.

Then the hard work began. With no starting point to guide me, I had to re-create my life from scratch. Like, literally. I upended my entire existence. I analyzed *everything*, down to whether or not I wanted or even liked bath mats. (I decided then that I didn't, but just over a decade later I have decided that now I do. Always changing). And for the first time in my life, *I* started living.

***

I'm sure there will be people, especially those in my field, who will read this and surmise that my story was simply one of trauma or codependence or low self-esteem, and certainly not the mysterious, eternal passing of memory from one being to another. They'll say I'm a girl who finally figured out how to love herself and that's that. And I'm sure there are many ways one might look at my story and provide a different narrative than what I'm giving here.

But I know differently. I know there's something in these historic drivers of behavior—the behaviors for which we can't find a starting point. There's something that lurks outside of the main-stream understanding of who we are and why we do what we do, something that plays out the same narratives over and over again. There's something not understood by most of us about the layers upon layers of choices we make, which are made for reasons we can't really even justify.

I didn't break out of my cycle because of some epiphany about loving myself more. To be frank, I still didn't. I had many, many miles of life to go before I knew in my heart of hearts that I deserved healthy love. No. On that rainy November day I still thought I didn't deserve a damn thing. Leaving wasn't about realizing I was better than all that I had endured from a relationship perspective. It wasn't about understanding the nature of love or trauma or worth. It wasn't even about finding myself, not really. Because I had no grand plan of where to go. I had no vision that I was motivated to see through. I just felt, somewhere in my core, that I had gotten to that moment in time through a whirlwind I didn't even under-stand, motivated by thoughts and feelings that led me to dead ends and discontent. It was not my life. And it had now become, quite simply, a die-or-completely-undo-it-all situation. In that moment, I decided to leap out of the existence I had, in a trust fall of hope of finding a truer one.

As I was beginning to gather notes for this book, I questioned my parents about their mind-set during my conception and pregnancy with me. Their words could have been me describing my feelings about my own life before that rainy run. It is not my place to tell the stories of others without their consent, and so my own family's tales will remain theirs to tell. But I can say with confidence that, with time, I was able to trace much of my own Imprint back, not just to my parents but back generations. I saw that I had spent my whole life in a cyclone of reliving some variation of my bloodline.

During the years that followed, I looked at my Imprint in detail.

I literally and figuratively cleaned house. I found that I had been carrying around in my life things that could be tossed altogether. And not just things. I mean ideas, thoughts, and notions. All things I could rid myself of because they never belonged to me in the first place. It's funny, to start life over while you're in the midst of it. Quite a messy undertaking in the end. And yet once you get off the ride you've been on from birth, it's like being able to see the world for the first time. It's like leaving Plato's cave.[18] The world is seen anew and there are a multitude of new options on how to live and behave. And when you don't have the boundaries of previous lives dictating which paths are open to you, you really do choose your own way.

After finding out that Bruce Willis is a ghost at the end of *The Sixth Sense*, I—like many of you—went back through the whole movie with a new way of viewing each scene. It's fascinating because during the first run-through of the movie I suspected something was amiss every now and again (like the scene where he and the mom are sitting across from each other but are just eerily silent), but I couldn't quite figure out what was going down. So when the reveal happens and M. Night (one of my favorite directors, by the by) does that little montage thing where he shows you where hints were placed, there's an "Oh, I *knew* something was off in that scene!" moment or two that pulls it all together and you're left with some satisfaction of knowing you weren't a complete moron, even if you didn't know *exactly* what was happening.

Finally seeing how the Imprint is impacting your life is a bit

---

[18] In Plato's allegory of the cave, from *The Republic*, a group of people in a cave face a blank wall. They watch shadows projected on the wall and see those shadows as their reality. The shadows, of course, are not accurate representations of the real world but simply are the only reality the viewers can perceive based on their limited view and senses. Someone who has advanced their thinking escapes the cave and sees the world for what it truly is.

like that. When this chapter of your story comes to its big reveal moment, when you realize how you've been influenced for so, so long, as you look back and inspect your life, you'll often find that clues were there, Easter eggs along the way.

For me, without a preconceived narrative of what pillars I needed to build my life around, I got to finally build one that made me happy. And I *am* happy. I *do* finally love myself, and I suspect that's because I am now living my life for me, not my ancestors. And there may be some of you reading this who knew me then. Before I had shed those lives and their influence. And I hope you see that I am not now who you knew then. Don't get me wrong. Even now, there are things from my past—traumas and hurts and nonadaptive behaviors—that I have to deal with still. Influences that I need to work to unlearn. But the process to adjust them has been so much more successful without all the noise from whatever was there before. The water is clear enough for me to finally see. I stopped living out my mother's and father's and grandparents' and great-grandparents' problems. I could never fix them anyway. And neither, I'm here to tell you, can you. So take control. Break free. We are, despite it all, still the captain of our ship, even if our ship is full of ghosts.

12

Tools

No one is free who has not obtained the empire of
himself. No man is free who cannot command himself.

—PYTHAGORAS

Our Imprints are carved onto our bones. They're etchings that,
like a spell, influence us outside of our conscious awareness,
prodding and nudging us into behaviors, decisions, and even dreams
that are not ours. And because they're ghosts—influences without
faces—we mistake them for ourselves and they can mold us in a way
that we subconsciously accept. Thus it can be really, maddeningly
tricky to try to see our Imprint. How can we tell if we are reliving the path of someone else or following our own way? It's likely
we'll never have a black-and-white answer. Again, our world exists
in the grey.

Many of us suffer from the idea that if it comes from our mind,
it must be "us." But as we've already noted, you have thoughts

before you think to have them, emotions that arise on their own. Just because we hear it in our heads and feel it in our hearts doesn't mean it's ours. So looking at our thoughts and emotions the same way we look at a flower on the side of the road can be extremely useful in understanding what comes from us and what is seemingly just showing up. My goal for you is to learn to live intentionally. To behave from choice rather than routine. And we can all stand to do quite a bit of that.

The following pages contain exercises to help you attempt to understand your Imprint, and also tips for how to move beyond it. Note that some of the exercises require knowledge of your birth family. I know that for some this is difficult or even impossible. Those of you for whom information about your birth family is incomplete or nonexistent can skip those exercises or choose to do just parts of them. Knowing your birth family isn't a requirement for healing. It can be helpful, yes. But don't be discouraged if you can't do all of these exercises. Even completing just one can open us up to seeing what ghosts live within ourselves.

While doing these exercises, really take the time to examine your thoughts, *especially* those that lead to action and choice. Why do you think that? Where does that thought come from? Why do we need to follow that line of thought? What happens if we thought a different way? Look around you. Really assess the life you're living, including the troubles you're having. If you remove the influence of those you don't want to follow, can you make room for the voices of those you do? Always ask the *why*. And then when you think you've found the why, ask again.

Oh, and be sure that you focus on each of the tools for at least thirty days. Research has shown that your brain needs that long to even *begin* to change behavior into muscle memory (Diamond, 1988). I find it's helpful to have a dedicated notebook to record all your work in. It's easier to see patterns when everything's all in one place, and it allows for you to take notes and spend time ruminating on what you find.

It is my sincere hope that one or more of these exercises will allow you to become less tethered to the choices of those who came before you. Or, if nothing else, to simply just be a better version of yourself.

I

The Experience Roadmap

When you look at a map, it's easier to see all the roads that lead to a given place. And when we create maps of our experiences alongside those of our family, we get a similar effect—it gives us the opportunity to see the paths we take that are headed to the same locations.

Instructions

Step 1: Create a genogram (see example). A genogram is a diagram illustrating who you and your family members are/were, how everyone is related, and major medical history (though we won't necessarily be focused on that part of the genogram here). Now, *officially*, there's an entire manual on how to set up a genogram, replete with dotted lines and triangles versus squares and so forth. And if this work excites you, I encourage you to dive deep and make yours as detailed you want. For everyone else, I'd like you to focus just on getting some high-level information onto paper. For our purposes, create your genogram using simple boxes or circles or whatever shape fills your inner creative, and try to list three to five major events and/or personality tidbits, such as "He was an ornery cuss."

Step 2: On another sheet of paper create a timeline for *just* your life (see example). Go year by year and try to remember all the major events and/or major feelings you had about those events or time periods. For instance, you might remember "feeling angsty" in your teen years, or the time you had to get stitches. If you have your family of origin available, you can ask them to create one of these for themselves. It is certainly not necessary, but it could provide better data in the end.

Step 3: Look at your genogram and compare that and your time-line to experiences and themes from your family of origin, including the ages at which events occur—even if the events themselves aren't similar.

Things to Note

- Try not to feel too worried if there's a great deal of similarity, or too much safety if there's none. This isn't meant to be a crystal ball; it doesn't predict an outcome. This is merely a tool to inspire curiosity about where you might be taking a path that mirrors the steps, decisions, or thought patterns of those who came before you, or where you may have tried to take a completely opposite path, invariably overcompensating and thus head down a road that still isn't true to you. All of this is information that you can use to understand some of the influences that may be impacting your decision-making.
- Do you cross paths a lot with a single individual? How does that feel?
- Are there intersectionalities between you and several people in your family history? On one item or many?
- Do other people in your family have similarities? What does that mean about them?
- If you have no similarities between yourself and your family of origin, what could that mean? Is there someone you're the complete opposite of?
- Looking at your timeline, what might someone outside of your inner circle think about the person whose life is represented

there? What are some major themes? What adjectives, both positive and negative, might someone state about the person?

- Circumstances play a role in how we see our own potential. Even as a small child, William, the city twin raised on the farm, was studious and drawn to learning. But his circumstances blocked some of his natural inclinations toward academics. Since learning where he's from and discovering he has more potential than he had led himself to believe he had, and since he's met his brother Jorge, he enrolled in law school in Bogota and now has political aspirations. Look to see whether you also have positive patterns—things from your or another ancestor's past that you can use as an anchor to propel yourself forward despite your circumstances.

GENOGRAM

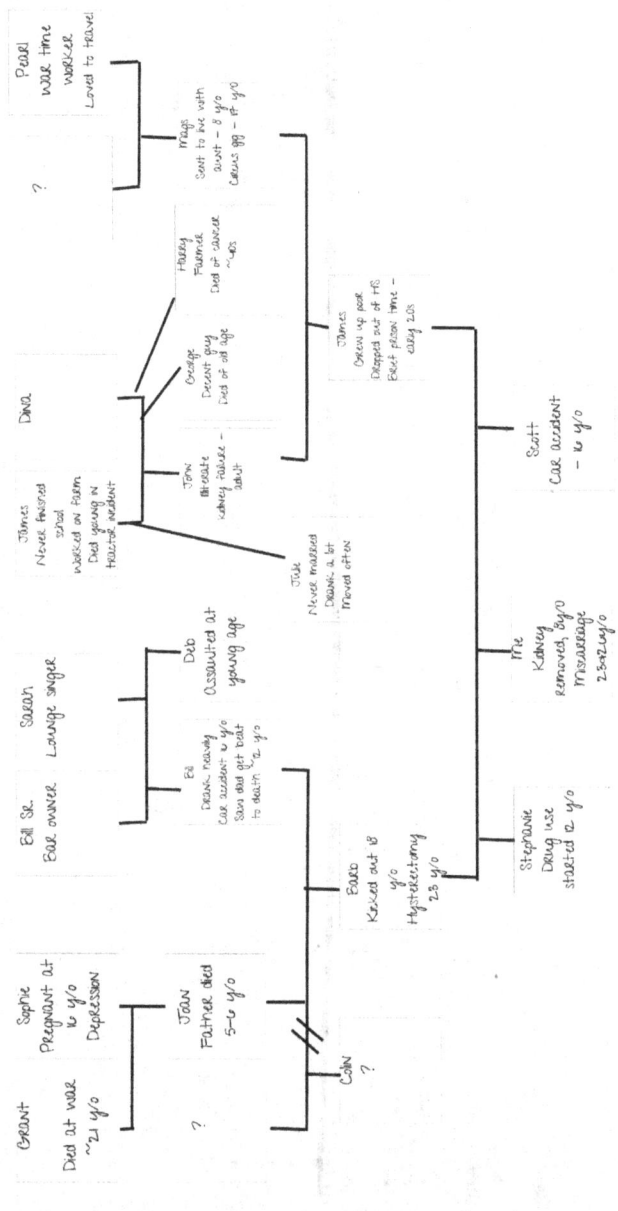

PERSONAL TIMELINE

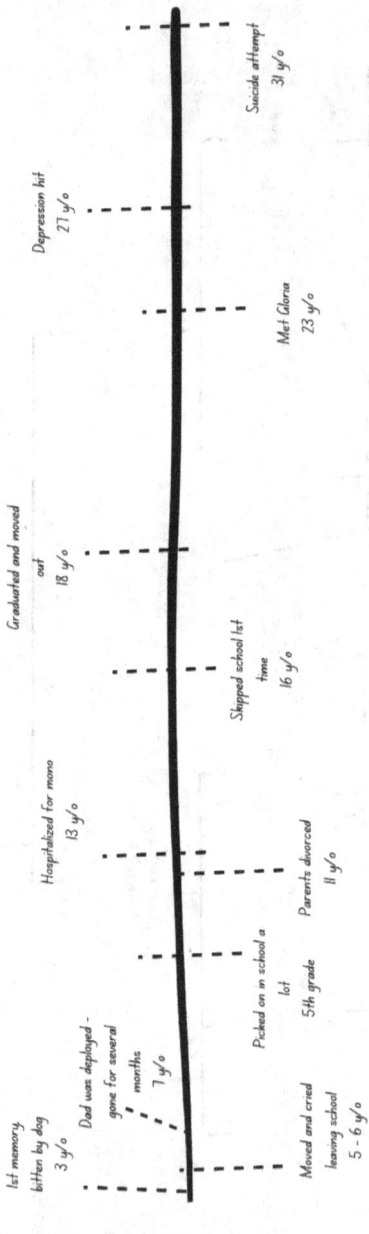

2

The Multiverse

In the 1990s show *Seinfeld*, the character of George is generally afflicted by poor decision-making, bad luck, and misery. In one episode, George's friend Jerry convinces George to do the opposite of everything he would normally do, because "if every instinct you have is wrong, then the opposite would have to be right." Now, I'm not suggesting every instinct you have is wrong. But for the sake of argument, let's say every decision you've made was . . . suspiciously under the influence. And if that's the case, what would the outcome have been if you had made some opposite choices? How does your story read if you had made the other decision in your life's crossroads?

Instructions

Step 1: Think of a turning point in your life. A moment where there was a choice to make and you had to pick one path instead of another. Create a flowchart that shows both options—the decision you made and an alternate decision that existed at the time. Got married? Not in this other life. Went to college to major in business? Let's go with your secret love of sculpting instead. Or maybe no college at all. Take your life all the way out to now, keeping a line going for what actually happened.

Step 2: Do a quick, knee-jerk review. Is there anything appealing about this other life? Any aspect that seems interesting? Anything that *feels* better?

Step 3: Pick another moment. And then another. Perhaps an earlier decision or something less monumental. Instead of buying that house in town, you opted for one in the country. Instead of getting two dogs, you opted for cats. Or maybe no animals at all. Play with all the iterations you can think of. Make as many universes as you can.

Step 4: Grab a few markers, crayons, or colored pencils. Pick two different colors and mark the events in your timeline that give you a firm "Yes, please!" feeling, along with the "Hell nah"s and the "Wish I never had"s. Then, determine a scale for everything in between. Your scale could look something like:

- Blue: Could see myself there in another life
- Yellow: Sounds intriguing
- Purple: I don't know why, but something about this feels interesting
- Orange: Didn't hate it

Step 5: Assess. What in those multiverses is appealing? Why? Are those aspects a part of your life now? Why or why not? What in your life do you wish you'd taken another path for? Can that choice be rectified in some way? If you're still living with that decision, why is it still part of your life? What choices might you have in the future?

Things to Note

- There's a tendency at first to want to "fix" all your current problems with a single change in one moment. And in some cases that could be possible. That said, it's equally possible that even if some of our bigger decisions were altered, our lives might not be wildly different than they've ended up. You're more than welcome to have a fully romanticized multiverse—the Happily Ever After one with all the bells and whistles. But be sure to make several other universes that, pragmatically, also could have occurred.

- You can list more than two choices. If one decision had multiple options you could have chosen, play all of them out.
- Avoid the temptation of what I refer to as "magical events," such as a decision to buy a lottery ticket and winning a million dollars—unless of course there was actually a moment in time where, had you bought the lottery ticket and played a particular set of numbers, you would have won. (And honestly, if that happened to you, my sincerest condolences because damn, that su-u-ucks.) This type of magical dreaming definitely has a place in the therapeutic process, but not for this exercise.
- In some instances, the alternate decision may not have changed a lot for you, or at least you can't think how. That's fine.
- The goal of this exercise is to see what choices *feel* good inside. What opportunities did we miss because we were too busy making choices that someone else made for us? What resonates in *our* soul versus that of the lives before us? Once you see what may have been, and dream a dream that might be different than the one you're living, you can see where, perhaps, corrections can be made to start living a life that's truer for *you*.

I've included an example on the next page. Since this book is in black and white, I've noted which colors the client chose for this exercise.

EXAMPLE

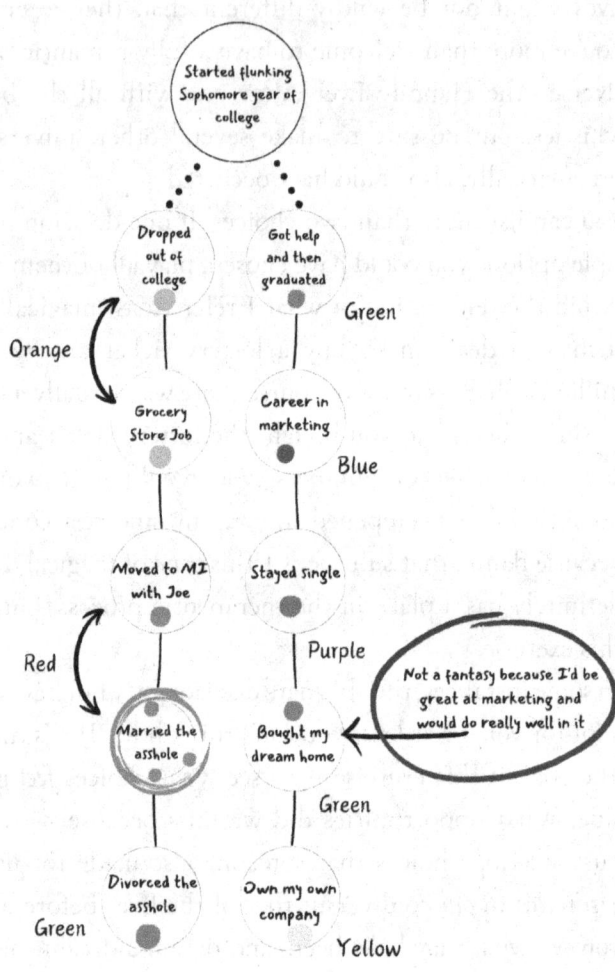

3

Ye Doth Protest Too Much

Do you have things that get to you and you don't really know why? An issue that you rage about no matter when it comes up? A type of scene in a movie that always makes you cry but you don't fully get why it pulls on your heart strings? If you notice that you have a reaction that feels slightly unwarranted—too big or too intense, for instance—or if certain scenarios incite emotions that seemingly come out of nowhere, you might be facing an Imprint. In *My Grandmother's Hands*, Resmaa Menakem (2017) noted something her mentor stated that sums this up well: "If something is hysterical, then it is usually historical." In other words, the urgency to do something is usually a great indication of how mired in the Imprint (and likely untrue) your thinking about the situation really is. Sometimes, when you go digging into the why, you realize there's nothing but a ghost.

Instructions

Step 1: Catalog any event in your day when your emotional reaction is large. It doesn't really matter at this moment whether you think your reaction was justified. We're just cataloging big feelings.

Step 2: Provide details. What was the root offense that occurred? For example, was someone running late to meet you and you lost it? What about the incident bothered you most?

Step 3: Find the earliest possible memory of a similar event.

In the sample event, for instance, when do you recall first being angered by someone being late? Now try to remember the scale of your reaction at the time. Was it softer, or were you just as upset then as you are now?

Step 4: Truly analyze the reaction you experienced in the current event. Obviously, if this was, say, the fourth time you found your partner texting someone in secret, you have an in-the-moment, real issue and don't need to look any further. But if you are about to shoot lasers out of your eyeballs because someone at the grocery store just cut in front of you, maybe we need to look at that. The output on paper could look something like this:

What happened?
A person cut in front of me at the grocery store.
How am I reacting, or how did I react?
If I could burn them with my thoughts, I would.
OK. So punishable by death. Was I in danger?
No.
Did this person harm me in any fundamental and real way?
No.
So why am I wishing death upon this person?
I don't like rude people?
Why?
Because they suck.
But they don't put me in harm's way.
I mean, I guess. But rude people can cause harm.
Ahhh. I see. And where does *that* "memory" come from?

Things to Note

- Try to avoid the pitfall of being sanctimonious here. You are not above being rude. You are not the pinnacle of a pure existence and humility. So saying, "I just believe being a good person with manners matters" or some other platitudinal thing isn't really helpful.
- Trace the line of questioning as far as you can. See if there's any substantive issue that could warrant such outrage. If it's just learned behavior from your parent—say, in the above example, perhaps a parent that always lamented the tragedy of rude (their definition of rude anyway) people—you can stop here. At least you know where the behavior comes from and don't have to carry it on.
- If you can't seem to find the source, you may be dealing with an Imprint. If this is the case, try step 4.

Step 4: When you're faced with the stimuli that gives you big feelings, force your brain to focus on the felt sense of that feeling. What I mean is, if your blood is boiling and your chest is tight, focus on those sensations—the physical ones. Do *not* focus on the mental story behind it. Don't ruminate on what you would say, on what you would do, or on what you wish they would do. Don't do anything but focus on the feelings within your body and catalog what you're experiencing.

Our brain will tell us we're justified as long as it's not under scrutiny. As soon as we really dissect what's happening or, as in this step, ignore the mental carousel in which we get trapped, we can let the emotion pass more quickly, giving us time to move on from any reactions that weren't ours to begin with.

EXAMPLE

Event	Reaction	Earliest Memory
A friend changed plans last minute	Total inner rage. All I could think was that I wanted to punish him. Couldn't let it go for hours.	I have no distinct memory of this from the past. Like, I know it's happened but I can't think of one specific instance.
Rose kept jumping around the living room even when I asked her to stop	I lost my shit. I yelled at her and sent her to her room. She cried.	I frankly never remember being allowed to play in the house, except our bedrooms and only then, as long as the noise didn't disturb my parents. If we were too loud, we were sent outside.

Thoughts on Event 1:

I really don't get it to be honest. I had a fully free day and the change didn't really effect

me negatively so I'm not really sure what this is about.

Thoughts on Event 2:

It's possible I just have a low tolerance for noise, or it's possible I just don't like it because

I never got to do it and I was never around it. Either way, I'm going to try to be more

patient when that happens at home and see where it goes.

4

Regulation, Mount Up

I like to ask my clients to rate their stress using a scale from 1 to 10, where 1 is the lowest stress, like you just woke up from a restful night's sleep, and 10 is "I can't imagine a more stressful situation," like you accidently pooped in your very white, very thin pants whilst performing on stage in front of a crowd of people. When we become increasingly stressed, like a 7 or higher on that scale, we revert back to automatic, knee-jerk-reactions. And when we're in this autopilot version of ourselves, we're not really going to do a lot of uncovering of what behaviors are ours versus those that we've inherited, especially if we're a walking powder keg. You can't do the necessary detective work of sorting and cataloging ferociously ingrained things if all your mental resources are being drained trying to not commit homicide. You must learn to regulate yourself —still the waters of your mind—so you can see with accuracy what is being reflected back.

Now, I could write a whole book on coping and self-soothing, but this book is not that one. So I'll give you a little something to start, and then, if you lack in this area, go find a professional to teach you more tools to learn self-regulation.

I like to separate coping skills from self-soothing skills, with an emphasis that you need both. Coping skills are what most folks typically think of when they're faced with the question of how to deal with stress. These are things that occur *after* the stressor has occurred and you are free to do whatever you need to do to lower your blood pressure. These are things like exercise, listening to music, taking a bath, journaling, and so on.

Self-soothing skills are what you do to calm yourself when you're *in the midst of* the stressor. When you're feeling *I can't escape, so how do I keep myself from completely melting down right here in this moment?* These are skills like breath work, mindfulness, body focus work, tapping, grounding techniques, and so on.

Instructions

Step 1: Make a list of your coping skills (see example). You should have at least five, with three in heavy rotation.

Step 2: Make a list of your self-soothing skills. You should have at least three, with one your go-to.

Things to Note

- If the ones you have don't work for you, ask yourself where you learned them from. Have you seen anyone in your life use these same tools? Do they work for them?
- If you don't have the minimum I noted above or if the ones you have that used to work no longer do, find a mental wellness professional and tell them you need a few sessions to learn more tools.

EXAMPLE

Soothing Skills	Coping Skills
Recite all 50 states	Gym
Try to balance on one foot	Coffee with friends
Deep breathing	Rage room
	Alone time
	Bake something
	Watch scary movies

5

Standard Operating Procedure

Often, we don't see how we resemble our primary caregivers because we're too busy focusing on how we're *not* like them. Blinded by a need to be different than they are or were, we miss opportunities to hunt out similarities that could be harmful. I once had a parent in my office who was painfully fixated on how they refused to withhold saying "I love you" to their children because, as a child themselves, their parents never said "I love you" and the hurt of that could never be shaken. But they assessed their parenting quality on this singular hurt and so they missed the *many* other ways they were repeating other, equally harmful behaviors. Our ability to fool ourselves into seeing what we want to see is one of our strongest mechanisms for survival.

Instructions

Step 1: Use the template below to create a standard operating procedure for each of your birth parents and one for yourself—so three in total. If you don't have access to your parents, have someone who knew them fill it out as best as possible, or if there's no one like that around, just tap into whatever memories you can find.

Step 2: Have your parents (or those proxies) do the same—one for themselves, one for you, and one for the other parent.

Things to Note

- Are there areas where there's a lot of overlap? Where are there differences?
- Why did the people write what they said about you? What experiences have they had interacting with you that would give them that information?
- Do you agree with what's there? If not, take a look at that. Are they way off base or are you denying information about yourself?

STANDARD OPERATING PROCEDURE

These are operating instructions for, well, you. Creating a cheat sheet that focuses on a smattering of key items about you can give you insight into things that could be influencing you outside of your normal awareness.

NAME	
KEY INFORMATION	What does this person think their purpose is?
	What do they think are their main responsibilities in life?
	Have you ever said, "They remind me so much of (someone in the family)?" Who and how?
BLOCKERS	How does this person cope with hardship?
	What does this person's behavior look like on their "bad" days?
MOTIVATIONS	What action / motivator will move this person to do things?
	What one thing makes this person tick?
SUPPORT NEEDED	How can someone best support this person when they're stressed?
	What mode of communication works best for this person?
OTHER	What is your strongest happy memory of this person?
	What is your strongest not happy memory of this person?

6

Fate or Folly

In his essay "Fate" (1857), Ralph Waldo Emerson discussed the idea that "Fate is nothing but the deeds committed in a prior state of existence." Exactly *which* existence, yours or those of your ancestors, is what we're focused on here. Are we moving forward in our own destiny (if there is such a thing), or are we living out the life of someone else?

One way we can work to identify whether we do what we do out of our fate or someone else's folly is by determining our biggest weakness. As we've already discussed, sometimes our biggest weakness is apparent at a very young age. It's a legacy handed down to us, a driving force that is so entwined in our DNA that we assume it's "just who we are" without trying to piece together how it came to be there in the first place. Now's our chance to do so.

Instructions

Step 1: Create a list of weaknesses (see example). Use whatever words make the most sense to you. You can search online for lists or make your own. I like to start clients off by looking at spiritual texts, as their propensity toward right and wrong behaviors provides readymade lists that tend to encapsulate the large majority of people's vices. Thus, you can find a list of weakness that will describe your "downfall" in almost every religion or spiritual leaning. The Hindu arishadvarga are the six enemies of the mind, the Christians have their seven deadly sins.[19] Even Buddhism has a set of things that can cloud your mind and prevent peace.

Step 2: Identify *your* biggest weakness. Take a look at the list you've created and think about it. Which of those items really stands out as something you struggle with? If you had to pick one, what would be the reason your character in a book about you could fail?

If you find you're having a hard time figuring out what your greatest weakness is, try the following:

- List your top one to three strengths and work backwards. What are the downsides to those strengths, the yang to the yin? The darker side of your most positive, beneficial qualities?
- Take a personality test. You can get as accurate as you want or just find some online quiz and see what resonates. If accuracy is what you're after, you might start with something a little more scientific. No personality test is without flaws, and some (the Myers-Briggs, for example) don't have a ton of validity despite every human resources organization in America thinking it's the gold standard. The Big 5 or HEXACO models would be better, though you must pay for each.
- Ask your friends and family. I'm hoping you have some loving people in your life who will tell you the unabashed truth in a compassionate way. Sometimes it might be hard to hear. But that outside perspective can be shockingly accurate. It's possible they've been dying to tell you some things, as it were, and may actually very much appreciate the opening to do so.

---

[19] In Jewish thought, a "sin" is not an offense against God but rather a missed opportunity to do the right thing. So if the words resonate with you but the idea of sin does not, try to think of sin in this context instead.

Step 3: Look at your life through the lens of that weakness. What choices have you made that are related to that vice? How have your decisions been impacted and influenced by this one feature? What might your life look like if this one trait didn't exist for you? What if the opposite were true—say, instead of being filled with pride you were filled beyond capacity with humility. What would life look like? How does it feel to see that alternate reality? What about that alternative life do you vibe with? What feels treacherous, and why?

Deep dive into this train of thought until you can look at that weakness from all angles.

Things to Note

- Weaknesses are not necessarily something to banish, and they're certainly not something to beat yourself up over. This is not an exercise in admonishing yourself. It's meant to inspire thought and awareness about what drives our decision-making and to note that influence on our lives. If you find yourself beating yourself up over this exercise, I encourage you to dive into shadow work with a mental wellness professional.

- Fate, should you believe in it, is an external force leading you on a path. So if you're spending a lot of time heading down avenues that were triggered by your weaknesses, you may be inadvertently sabotaging yourself. And even if you're completely atheist or believe in chaos theory or that there is no path, you still owe it to yourself to figure out just how much your biggest weakness is influencing your life. Because no matter what, whatever path you should or could be on, the most successful, healthy version of that will be one where your strengths and weaknesses are successfully balanced.

EXAMPLE

Attachment?

~~Vanity~~

~~Anger~~

(Jealousy)

~~Ignorance~~

~~Desire~~

~~Aversion~~

~~Arrogance~~

~~Greed~~

~~Gluttony~~

~~Sloth~~

7

Personality Trait Slider

It's helpful to see what drivers might be unknowingly influencing behavior when we look at how aligned we are to the traits of our primary caregivers.

Instructions

Step 1: Split a piece of paper in half. Label one side for your mother and the other for your father. If you only had one of those people in your life growing up, no need to add the other.

Step 2: For each side, list the dominant traits of that parent. Note that we're going for dominant here, so only list the things that are undeniably them. People are complex humans, and if we tried to list every single trait a person holds, we would fill pages. You're aiming for five to ten traits here. It can help to do a quick internet search for a list of both positive and negative traits as a starting point.

Step 3: Draw a line from each identified trait to the other side of each person's box and write the opposite of that trait (see example). It's important to note that our view of language is very personal and mired in context. I find it useful to grab a dictionary to find just the right word to describe the opposite that is based on the context surrounding the word you used. For instance, if you said your father was fickle because he would show up sometimes but not others, then a good opposite might be *reliable*. However, if you wrote that your father was fickle because he could never make up his mind on things, you might choose the opposite of *certain* or even *persistent* instead.

Step 4: Using a crayon or marker, mark with a dot where *you* fall on each trait scale.

Step 5: Draw a line down what is roughly the middle of the set of lines.

Step 6: Assess what you see. How close are you to the traits of your parents? Did you align with one parent in particular? Did you go to the complete opposite extreme in some or even all cases? Any traits where you're on the extremes of either end could signify to you that there's something deep down moving your behavior. Your goal is to try to be more in the middle (again, not the farthermost opposite), so ask yourself what you can do to get closer to that balanced state. Moving toward equilibrium could allow you to remove the influences that are pushing you in a polarized direction.

Things to Note

- As with all of these exercises, be honest. Lying to yourself does no good.
- It is not necessary to become filled with guilt and try to find positive things to "balance" negative traits, or to downplay negative traits. If your mother was a relentless nag, let it be known. No one has to see this but you, and so whatever obligation you may feel to try to be sure people know the person wasn't all bad or wasn't terrible doesn't need to come into play. You're not submitting this as their eulogy—it's for data. Make that data accurate.
- On any scale where you're in that middle area from step 5, the influence of those traits is more likely to be yours and yours alone. However, if you're on an end, that could be significant, especially if you're on the same end as your parent.

- Don't be fooled by thinking that being on the opposite end means you're not being influenced by the Imprint. We often put too much emphasis on *not* having a trait because we secretly *are* that thing, so if you find yourself on the total opposite end of the scale, it could be because you're pushing hard to convince yourself you're not something you actually feel deep inside.

EXAMPLE

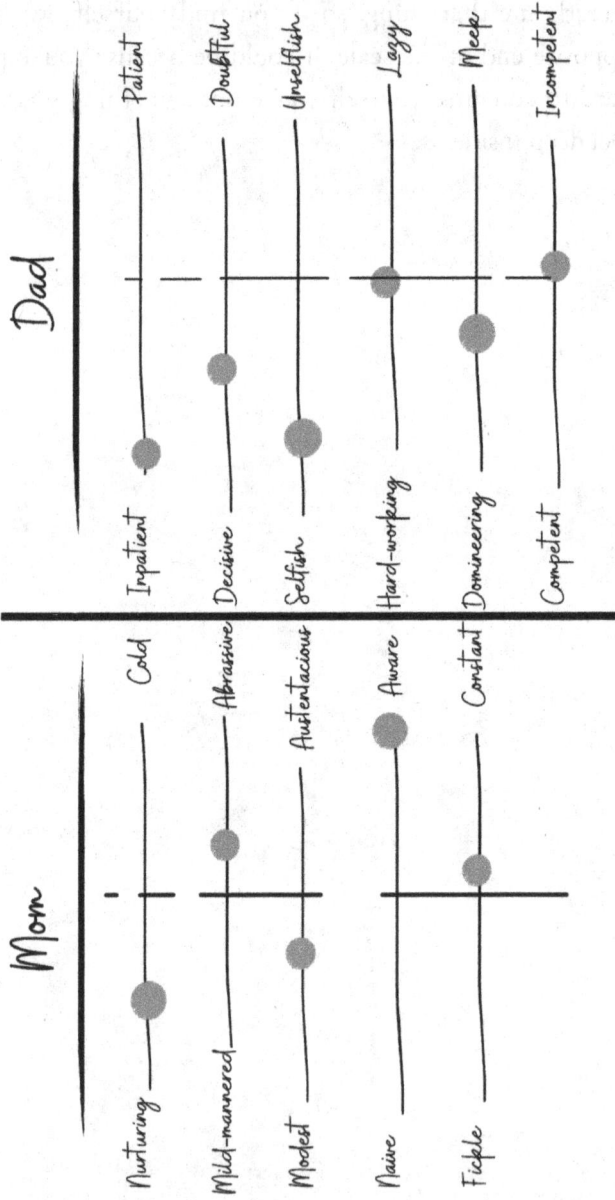

8

Dominant versus Nondominant Handwriting

Our mind has way of creating a shield to guard us from ourselves. But sometimes we can lessen the shield by dedicating some mental resources to a task that requires concentration. Kind of like how accidently banging your head against something hard will distract you from whatever turmoil you may have been pondering just moments before. Luckily, we don't have to induce pain to get the same results.

Instructions

Step 1: Get a piece of paper and divide it in half lengthwise.

Step 2: Have your dominant hand pose a question to yourself, such as "Is it true I will never find true love?" Write this question down on the same side of the paper—so if you normally write with your right hand, you'll write your question at the top of the right side of the page.

Step 3: Whatever you hear yourself think back—the first thing that pops into your head—use your non-dominant hand to write that retort down on the other side of the paper. Then write down the response to that with your dominant hand, and so on and so forth (see example). Be quick about it—do not to allow yourself to edit what gets written. The conversation is over when your mind is blank and you "hear" no further retorts from either side.

Things to Note

- This exercise is about removing influenced and/or distortive thinking that can come across in our thought patterns. By forcing your left and right brains to converse in rapid-fire fashion, you help loosen up the filter that prevents you from seeing what's underneath automatic thoughts. There are times in which our Imprint shields us from taking an honest look at a situation, and so distracting our brain's filters can be the key to seeing what is true.
- Sometimes the very first thing we think after a sentence is a nonsensical one. *Still write it down.* If you filter that one, then you'll be on guard to filter other thoughts. And we don't want to filter *any* of the thoughts that might be guiding us to what is at the root of where we are.

EXAMPLE

	Should I stay at my job?
D'uh	
	That's not helpfull
Well of course you should stay.	
	But why?
Because money	
	Yea, but that can't be all there is.
But it is	
	I don't accept that
what else is there??	
	HAPPINESS?!
Where is there room for that?	
	I don't really know
That's kinda sad	
	It really is
Maybe we should fix that	
	You know, we really should
So quit	
	Yea, I really should

9

Quantum Attention

Yet another intriguing aspect of quantum physics comes from an experiment reported by the Weizmann Institute of Science (1998). Electrons can behave as either a particle or a wave, and the Weizmann experiment showed that electrons changed type depending on the mind-set and expectations of the person watching it. The mere act of observation affected what the particle did. It raises the question, Can what we think and watch change what occurs in our own lives? Now, before all the science folks roll their eyes, let me add the disclaimer that the study does not in any way prove that a person can significantly alter their reality just by thinking about it.

But with all that said, I do think there's something here we can use. In 1949, psychologist Donald Hebb famously stated, "Neurons that fire together, wire together." By choosing to shift our focus to certain things in our brain, we can gain the ability to form memories and associations of our own choosing, which can, in time and in ways we don't fully understand, impact what is happening in our reality. What's more, in doing so we start to change our brain, and with that, we affect a host of other things like mirror neurons, which have a large role in empathy, understanding, and even predictive abilities, and other data stored at the cellular level (Keysers and Gazzola, 2014).

For instance, let's say you choose to focus more on understanding other people's behavior. To do this, you might go to a café each day and just people-watch. After focusing on this effort for a while, your brain starts to wire together motions and subsequent actions, making you better at predicting the behavioral patterns of others. Goal achieved. But as an added bonus, the brains of the people close to you subconsciously recognize your increased awareness (the fancy word for this is *attunement*), and as a result they start to behave more positively with you. They may increase their emotional vulnerability or start to act in a more positive way, and thus better opportunities show up in your life because your connection to others has been strengthened.

Before we dive into the exercise, I need to take a moment and be clear. The "If you will it, it will happen" and "Positive thoughts lead to a positive life" manifestation talk can do a lot of harm and result in a lot of victim blaming if we're not careful. If we lean too far into this line of thinking, we can get all too very close to the idea that bad things in life are there because you just aren't positive enough. It starts to get a little to near the idea that, if your life is not wonderful, you're just not wanting it enough. This reeks of the same religious trauma–causing notion that if you just prayed hard enough or better, or were in God's favor, bad things wouldn't happen. Nobody—and I do mean nobody—needs to hear that, and I'm pretty sure children who are kidnapped, murdered, and other-wise living in trauma aren't there because they're just not imagining a good life hard enough.

We cannot control all of our life purely by desire. We cannot manifest away systemic racism or misogyny or injustice. Thinking we can ignores that there is chaos and randomness and that life isn't fully in our hands. It also gives people an excuse to avoid actually doing something about those larger problems. If you believe every-one can just manifest their way to riches and out of poverty, you're going to be far less inclined to actually assist in dismantling systems of poverty within your community. So like, don't do that.

OK. On to the exercise!

Instructions

Step 1: Identify the trouble spots in your thinking and mood. Do you hate mornings? Have crappy relationships? Struggle to find patience at your kids' bedtime? Pick one that you wish you didn't feel. Rank it on a scale of *Miserable* to *Bearable*.

Step 2: Shift your focus around those events. If you hate mornings, focus on all the positive things a morning can bring. Force yourself to look outside and count as many pretty things as you can and sit with it—really sit with it. Listen to the sounds around you and try to find beauty there. The goal here isn't "Positivity wins!" We're not trying to blow sunshine up your butt. But we're trying to retrain neurons to fire together in a way they didn't before—to fundamentally change your brain. You can't hike on a new path if you keep going down the one from the day before.

Step 3: Do this for at least thirty days and then mark your relationship with that same thing (see example). Did it improve? If not, what could you do differently? What other areas could you focus on?

Things to Note

- Patterns of thinking wear deep grooves in our brain, regardless of where they come from. You choosing to bushwhack a new path instead of heading down that same, well-worn road you have for years (or decades) will be hard, and you're not going to want to do this. Everything is going to tell you to go back to the worn path. But once you get the new path cleared enough, which occurs when we do something consistently for an ample period of time, it *will* become more comfortable. It will start to feel normal.

- Depending on how long you've been walking the other path, the clearing itself might take you longer than it takes someone else. That's fine. This isn't a race.
- After you've done this activity with things that bother you, turn it onto yourself. How we see ourselves can impact the life we lead. For example, believing you have innate qualities that make you good or bad at something—called "entity theories"—can change the way you perform on that task (Severns, 2012). A study led by a researcher from the University of Illinois at Urbana–Champaign suggested that children can adopt beliefs from information they hear about their gender, and presumably about other characteristics, such as age, ethnicity, and the like (Cimpian et al., 2012). For instance, a girl who hears that "girls are bad at math" can internalize that message and do worse at math because of it. In the study, 144 children played a game. After the first round, the adult leading the experiment told some children that the other-gender group was successful at the game—so girls heard "Boys are good at this game." A second group was told about individuals' skills, such as "That girl is good at this game." And a third group received no message. Then the children played another, more difficult round of the game. The scores of those who were given the gender prompts fell by an average of 12.8%. By contrast, children who were told about another individual child's success or failure stayed about the same, and scores fell 2.9% among the kids who heard nothing.

EXAMPLE

BEARABLE — **THINGS THAT SUCK** — **KILL ME NOW**

Running late

Plans changing last minute

Early morning conversations/work needing to be done

Chewing sounds

- Have wanted to learn better how to go with the flow
- Could be better than what was planned
- What if like, I would've had something go crazy wrong in the original plan
- Potential new experiences
- I still get to hang with the people I wanted to
- In some cases, I get cancelled plans which often a total win

IO

Take a Quest

Sometimes we have to get outside ourselves to see ourselves clearly. The whole "You can't see the forest through the trees" adage. Sometimes, to really hear what our internal voices are telling us, we need to get out of the environment that drowns them out.

Changing your life is about the *deliberate* act of doing something. Changing the cycle depends on us making a choice to rail against everything inside of us that is pushing us in a direction. It is counter to everything we find comfortable and goes against everything we feel is "us." But how can we know who we are? We've never had a chance to find out because we've been hurling ever forward on a trajectory that started before we were born. We have been sucked into the idea of fate, without taking into account what fate might actually be. For instance, what if fate is simply the hard push from these ghost remnants we've been discussing that are in reality just blocking the true us? Not a thing meant for us at all?

There are countless quest types across culture and time. Those established quests vary in intensity, length, and the time of life at which they are taken, but in the end they serve as a tool to help someone find themselves and their life's direction. And what are we trying to do here but to find ourselves outside the noise of the ghosts of our ancestors? What do we need but to find a direction separate from the repeated lives of those who came before us?

One of the core tenets of a quest is that the quester spends time alone in nature in search of a personal vision. It would be beneficial to plan for several days for your quest—two to three days and nights, preferably in wilderness—and a few days of incorporation.

Step 1: During the preparation, you are readied to physically, psychologically, mentally, and spiritually benefit from the experience of your quest, such as knowing how you will eat while you're out on your quest and what clothes you will need.

Step 2: The experience involves time alone in a natural place (allowing for solitude), possible fasting (or something that brings on the sensation of emptiness), exposure to the elements (providing vulnerability), and self-reliance (tapping into self-trust).

Step 3: Upon return, head to your local mental wellness person or a trusted friend group for the sharing of stories and processing of the emotions and thoughts you encountered. Reflect upon the significant lessons of your story, and then challenge yourself to use what you learned and to live life with this new perspective.

Things to Note

- The documented benefits of spending time in nature include but are not limited to stress reduction, an increase in fascination and appreciation for the environment, a sense of competence and self-esteem balanced with a sense of trust in oneself (what we call 'agency') and the world, a more mature sense of empathy and care for others. Thus, even if you don't want to find your Imprint, a quest of this nature can have amazing benefits.
- There are companies that provide services to help people embark on these types of quests. It could be extremely beneficial to utilize that kind of entity if this is your first time embarking on this type of thing. That said, do your research carefully to ensure you're going with a reputable company.

No man can know where he is going unless he knows exactly where he has been and exactly how he arrived at his present place.

—MAYA ANGELOU

I would be remiss, given my line of work, to not mention how talking to someone—a professional who focuses on mental wellness —can help with the task of living a truly authentic life. A research group in the U.S. and the Netherlands worked with a group of veterans to look for associations among DNA, PTSD, combat-related trauma, and response to psychotherapy. Participants in the study had been deployed at least once for at least four months, and some had been diagnosed with PTSD. Those with PTSD were treated with either eye movement desensitization and processing (EMDR) or trauma-focused cognitive behavioral therapy (TF-CBT), and a group of those same vets also was being treated with various medications (e.g., antidepressants and sedatives). Not surprisingly, treating PTSD, no matter how, was effective, with just under half of the veterans in remission at the completion of the study (Fagan, 2019; Vinkers et al., 2021).

What was interesting was that EMDR was associated with a small but significant difference in the actual epigenetics of the vets that underwent that treatment. In those vets, one of the gene regions that appears to govern PTSD development and recovery started acting differently, both during and after treatment. And that same gene region seemed to be heavily activated by therapy, resulting in reduced PTSD symptoms and increased remission. Wellness work can quite literally help you down to your very core.

And you don't need to identify as having trauma to reach out to someone. Self-improvement is a path with no end. Even if we're living a decently contented existence, it never hurts to poke around in the stores of our being to see how things are doing. We are never stagnant, and life experiences continue to shape our thoughts and behaviors. It's important that we never close the door to checking in on ourselves—on assessing if who we are today still works for us and our life in the present.

13

The Unhaunted Mind

"And if I could," my father wrote to me,
huge as a bear himself, when I was younger,
"I would dower you with experience, without experience."
And I, in my turn, would pass that on to you.
But we make our own mistakes. We sleep unwisely.

—NEIL GAIMAN, "LOCKS"

The Imprint is your unintentional inheritance. It's the inter-generational transference of other's lives – their experiences, memories, thoughts, feelings, and even actions. It's your ancestors guiding you in ways you likely don't yet notice. For some people, the Imprint feels like an influence to become people they didn't set out to be, even pushing many of them to become a person they had actively tried with all their might not to become. For others, the Imprint is a force they feel guides them—an influence "bigger" than them but somehow *of* them. Upon a few, the Imprint bestows interests, actions, or thoughts that feel like a muse. All these reactions make sense. The Imprint is made of so many lives. Some of them will be supportive. Some will not. And so many more will be both.

I'm sure that the original intent of the Imprint's creation—by what force would be pure conjecture—was to help us, to give us information we might need to survive a life like the ones lived before us. And as I've mentioned, the Imprint is, in and of itself, both helpful and hurtful. After all, our ancestors give us more than just their wounds. In its deepest recesses, in its most profound details, it means we each carry the knowledge of centuries of living. We carry remnants of the earliest of human experiences, which in turn means each of us has the ability to know more than what we think we do, to have, through the memories of others, knowledge of the world that doesn't require us to have lived a life that resulted in that knowledge. The built-in armor to fight off threats that we no longer see. The ways to harmony, and of peace. And how beautiful it is to realize that we are never alone. We never have been. There is, in each of us, a vast history of ancestors by our side.

But the Imprint is memories transmitted without context. It's information projected in a vacuum. As such, we have no way of tracing back an emotion or thought that stems from the Imprint, nor can we expect to be able to adequately process it. Thus, we have to see the Imprint as information, not a truth that we need to act on. Just as there is no need to re-create the recipes by the grandmother who oversugars everything because in her time she believed the advertising that sugar could help you lose weight. And just as there is no need to heed the ramblings of a grandfather who insists that an entire country of people is flawed because, during his years, he suffered through time at war. Their experiences are based on their time and their knowledge. They are not always truthful in our time with our knowledge. We need to stop letting the ghosts guide us in ways that don't serve the person we need to become.

The Imprint is full of experiences, which means that even as it can be a source of wisdom it's also full of unfinished business and axes to grind. It is influencing you to live out parts of lives that others couldn't, to resolve debts left unsettled, to ruminate on things with which others couldn't find peace in their minds.

It's time to stop letting our ghosts give us unhealthy drives and unadaptable ways of living. Because by influencing us, they impact everyone—our selves, our families, our society. We cannot exist without one another. And if there's no other reason to unburden yourself from your Imprint, do it to help others. Self-improvement is not just about making us better but also about improving our communities. We fix ourselves so we can stop recreating the same broken world.

And I admit, that's hard to do. It's so much easier to just keep stumbling forward with the momentum that has pushed you here. After all, to stay as we are is easy. Set in motion, we continue in motion. We obey a compulsion to keep going, to repeat the same life over and over and over until something stops the momentum. Hell, most people don't want to attempt change because what they're doing feels normal—it feels "right"—simply because it's what always has been. Sure, we might break a cycle here or there—be the first of your family to finish college, commit to a gentler type of parenting. And those things are absolutely wonderful and deserve your self-gratitude and pride. But even in the midst of those seemingly large changes, more often than not the larger narrative stays the same, our lives still echo from our family trees.

After my proverbial cliff-jump moment, one of the many changes I made was a commitment to truth-telling. Specializing in trauma work, I made the decision that I never want to lie to my children. And children, being the quintessential secret-spillers, are a great way to keep yourself honest about honesty. Now, a *lot* of people tell me they agree with being honest, that is until their lives give them reasons to tell lies, especially the seemingly harmless ones. But a commitment to truth-telling means I don't tell you things will be OK when they won't be. I don't sell an idea of Santa Claus or the tooth fairy. I don't tell you it's fine when it's not. And I try, albeit sometimes in vain, to avoid lying to the person we all lie to the most—ourselves.

When I made that choice to be truthful, it forced me to change an entire life of behavior. And what's more, it forced me to shift course quickly. I was a person who lied to avoid pain and hurt and overall discomfort. It was never malicious. It was always done to keep the peace. The decision shook my fundamentals—the way I thought and acted had to adjust. I couldn't claim "that's just me" in the face of this newly chosen identity. I couldn't make my old mold fit. It *forced* me to act from a place of newness. And honestly, I think that's what's necessary.

I'm not saying we have to give up *everything* we are now. For instance, I had children when I made that leap into the unknown, and I would never have cut myself off from them. What's more, some of you reading this already have really wonderful lives. You're happy with who you are and what's around you. And if you're genuinely content, why would you want to change that?

But for everything we keep, we add an element of complexity to being able to let the old go. And if we aren't willing to even explore upending what we have—to analyze the choices that got us here and kept us from a different life—then how can we ever truly know we're living a unique, intentional existence?

Our brains are designed to reduce stress by finding comfort in the "normal," even if that normal is unhealthy or unadaptable. If I ate a doughnut every day for ten years and then tried to stop due to a health issue, my entire being would crave that doughnut because I'd been doing it for so damn long, even if it could kill me. We're simply hardwired to resist change. And if that change can be easily undone, if there is an "easy" button enabling us to go back to the old way of doing things, it makes change, especially change that disrupts a bad habit, one hundred times harder.

There are many reasons to keep particular elements of our lives. We don't need to burn it *all* down. All I'm asking is that we each pause and take the time to assess who the *I* of the self actually is. I certainly don't want to be a prisoner of forces influencing me, regardless of whether those forces are coming from inside or outside of myself, and I suspect you don't either. I want to live my own life, unhindered by the wants of someone who is not me. And in order to do that, we need to truly and truthfully do a bit of self-exploration.

If we accept that human beings came from a few and grew to the staggering billions we are now, it also means that most of us have at least some of the same Imprints. After all, doppelgängers and people who have similar features are simply part of our family tree that split off long ago. A study published in the journal *Cell Reports* found that people with very similar faces not only share many of the same genes but also tend to have similar lifestyles, with similarities shown in both life history and education levels (Joshi et al., 2022).

And in the end, if we're all just reliving the same few stories over and over, the weird coincidences we come across start to make a bit more sense. In the James brothers' case, both sets of parents independently named their child James and called him Jim. But then, both families went on to adopt another child, and both named that new child Larry (Chen, 1979). Thus, the parents too had some sort of connection—something that made them make similar choices in their own lives.

You ever have those times when similarities in lives keep popping up? The "OMG my friend and I were just saying that too!" moments? The times you find yourself facing eerily similar themes threading your life? People dying in threes. Four of your friends experiencing heartache around the same time. Consistency happening on a large, life-size scale?

I was once talking to a close friend and was describing persistent feelings of being not good enough. I was lamenting how frustrating it is to know what you're supposed to do but to be unable to escape the fear of rejection. Four hours later, I was seeing a client who had had enough. They then lamented, using almost the exact words I had used with my friend, how frustrating it is to know what you're supposed to do but to be unable to escape the fear of rejection. Then, two days later, a person in one of the online groups I participate in felt the need to share. The topic? They described persistent feelings of being not good enough. They then lamented, using almost the exact same words (you see the theme here), how frustrating it is to know what you're supposed to do but to be unable to escape the fear of rejection.

Sometimes it feels like everybody's going through the same thing. And given what we know about the Imprint, maybe it's true. If our Imprints are from all of our ancestors, and each person here on earth has the same ancestors, well, maybe we're all just echoes of the very same thing. That endless, eternal ripple.

In *The Absolution of Roberto Acestes Laing*, Nicholas Rombes wrote:

> In college I had a physics professor who wrote the date and time in red marker on a sheet of white paper and then lit the paper on fire and placed it on a metallic mesh basket on the lab table where it burned to ashes. He asked us whether or not the information on the paper was destroyed and not recoverable, and of course we were wrong, because physics tells us that information is never lost, not even in a black hole, and that what is seemingly destroyed is, in fact, retrievable. In that burning paper the markings of ink on the page are preserved in the way the

flame flickers and the smoke curls. Wildly distorted to the point of chaos, the information is nonetheless not dead. Nothing, really, dies. Nothing dies. Nothing dies. (p. 36)

Nothing dies indeed. But we certainly don't need to keep dragging around the past either. It's time to live looking forward.

- Release the fears given to you that were meant to protect you but instead maintain systems of oppression.
- Release the angers given to you that were meant to avenge but instead maintain systems of conflict and war.
- Release the griefs given to you that were meant to honor but instead maintain systems of distress.
- Embrace the wisdom given to you about connection, learning that community equals safety, and go find your people.
- Embrace the wisdom given to you about love, that we protect ourselves by protecting one another, and find the strengths hidden within.
- Embrace the wisdom given to you about knowledge, that the passing down of information is vital to growth, and find the value of discovery.

Live life as it is now, instead of how it always has been. Heal the wounds from your experiences and release those that aren't yours. Build community. Discover an authentic and honest version of yourself. Take the time now, here, with these words and in this moment, to commit that when *you* die, what is left is a life that you can claim was truly yours. An intentional existence. One that lets your ancestors, and their Imprints upon you, finally and forever rest. And in doing so, dawns—both quite figuratively and literally—a whole new age of existence.

References

Abler, Thomas S. (1980). Iroquois cannibalism: Fact not fiction." *Ethnohistory, 27*(4): 309–316. https://doi.org/10.2307/481728

Afilalo, R. R. (Trans.). (n.d.). *Shaar Hagilgulim: Gate of Reincarnations.* https://www.academia.edu/22015256/Shaar_Hagilgulim_Gate_of_Reincarnations

Albarracín, D., and Wyer, R. S. Jr. (2000). The cognitive impact of past behavior: Influences on beliefs, attitudes, and future behavioral decisions. *Journal of Personality and Social Psychology, 79*(1): 5–22. https://doi.org/10.1037//0022-3514.79.1.5

Ashwell, A. R. (1880–1882). *Life of the Right Reverend Samuel Wilberforce, D.D., lord bishop of Oxford and afterwards of Winchester, with selections from his diaries and correspondence.* 3 volumes. John Murray.

Bauer, Ann Z., Swan, Shanna H., Kriebel, David, Liew, Zeyan, Taylor, Hugh S., Bornehag, Carl-Gustaf, Andrade, Anderson M., Olsen, Jørn, Jensen, Rigmor H., Mitchell, Rod T., Skakkebaek, Niels E., Jégou, Bernard, and Kristensen, David M. (2021). Paracetamol use during pregnancy—a call for precautionary action. *Nature Reviews Endocrinology, 17*: 757–766. https://doi.org/10.1038/s41574-021-00553-7

Bhikkhu, Thanissaro. (Trans.) (2003). Maha-hatthipadopama Sutta: The great elephant footprint simile. https://www.accesstoinsight.org/tipitaka/mn/mn.028.than.html

Bjornsson, H. T., Sigurdsson, M. I., Fallin, M. D., Irizarry, R. A., Aspelund, T., Cui, H., Yu, W., Rongione, M. A., Ekström, T. J., Harris, T. B., Launer, L. J., Eiriksdottir, G., Leppert, M. F., Sapienza, C., Gudnason, V., & Feinberg, A. P. (2008). Intra-individual change over time in DNA methylation with familial clustering. *JAMA, 299*(24), 2877–2883. https://doi.org/10.1001/jama.299.24.2877

Blum, Brian. (2020). Can you pass along genetic changes from your environment? *Israel21c* (September 3). https://www.israel21c.org/can-you-pass-along-genetic-changes-from-your-environment

Brasfield, M. (2013). Mother's intuition: Why we should follow our "gut feelings." *Today.com* (April 18). https://www.today.com/parents/mothers-intuition-why-we-should-follow-our-gut-feelings-1c9504706

Chen, E. (1979). Twins reared apart: A living lab. *New York Times* (December 9). https://www.nytimes.com/1979/12/09/archives/twins-reared-apart-a-living-lab.html

Cimpian, A., Mu, Y., & Erickson, L. C. (2012). Who is good at this game? Linking an activity to a social category undermines children's achievement. *Psychological Science, 23*(5): 533–541. https://doi.org/10.1177/0956797611429803

Conover, Emily. (2019). An experiment hints at quantum entanglement inside protons. *ScienceNews* (May 17). https://www.sciencenews.org/article/experiment-hints-quantum-entanglement-inside-protons

Cossart, Y. E. (1967). Genetic marker studies of poliovirus: I. Natural variation. *Journal of Hygiene, 65*(1): 65–76. https://doi.org/10.1017/S002217240004554X

Curry, A. (2019). Parents' emotional trauma may change their children's biology: Studies in mice show how. *Science* (July 18). https://www.sciencemag.org/news/2019/07/parents-emotional-trauma-may-change-their-children-s-biology-studies-mice-show-how

Deichmann, Ute. (2016). Epigenetics: The origins and evolution of a fashionable topic. *Developmental Biology, 416*(1): 249–254. https://doi.org/10.1016/j.ydbio.2016.06.005

DenHoed, Andrea. (2016). The forgotten lessons of the American eugenics movement. *New Yorker* (April 27). https://www.newyorker.com/books/page-turner/the-forgotten-lessons-of-the-american-eugenics-movement

Diamond, M. C. (1988). *Enriching heredity: The impact of the environment on the anatomy of the brain.* The Free Press.

Dickler, J. (2022). Unrelenting inflation is driving up costs, leaving more Americans living paycheck to paycheck. *CNBC* (August 1). https://www.cnbc.com/2022/08/01/as-inflation-surges-more-americans-are-living-paycheck-to-paycheck.html

Dolan, M. (2012). The gruesome history of eating corpses as medicine. *Smithsonian Magazine* (May 6). https://www.smithsonianmag.com/history/the-gruesome-history-of-eating-corpses-as-medicine-82360284

Dworin, Jack, and Wyant, Oakley. (1957). Authoritarian patterns in the mothers of schizophrenics. *Journal of Clinical Psychology, 13*: 332–338.

Esselmann, Samantha Ancona. (2020). What it means to have "Native American DNA." *23andMe blog* (November 20). https://blog.23andme.com/articles/native-american-dna

Fagan, Abigail. (2019). Can psychotherapy reverse post-traumatic epigenetic changes?. *Psychology Today* (October 29). https://www.psychologytoday.com/us/blog/psychiatry-the-people/201910/can-psychotherapy-reverse-post-traumatic-epigenetic-changes

Fall, Tove, Kuja-Halkola, Ralf, Dobney, Keith, Westgarth, Carri, & Magnusson, Patrik K. E. (2019). Evidence of large genetic influences on dog ownership in the Swedish Twin Registry has implications for understanding domestication and health associations. *Scientific Reports, 9* (7554).

Foer, J. (2011). *Moonwalking with Einstein.* Penguin.

Fordham News. (2018). In Colombia, a curious case of mixed-up twins and brotherly love. *Fordham Magazine* (August 30). https://news.fordham.edu/fordham-magazine/in-colombia-a-curious-case-of-mixed-up-twins-and-brotherly-love

Gapp, K., Bohacek, J., Grossmann, J. Brunner, A. M., Manuella, F., Nanni, P., and Mansuy, I. M. (2016). Potential of environmental enrichment to prevent transgenerational effects of paternal trauma. *Neuropsychopharmacology, 41*: 2749–2758. https://doi.org/10.1038/npp.2016.87

Garrett-Bakelman, Francine E., et al. (2019). The NASA twins study: A multidimensional analysis of a year-long human spaceflight. *Science, 364*(6436). https://doi.org/10.1126/science.aau8650

Georgiades, E., Klissouras, V., Baulch, J., Wang, G., and Pitsiladis, Y. (2017). Why nature prevails over nurture in the making of the elite athlete. *BMC Genomics, 18* (Suppl. 8): 835. https://doi.org/10.1186/s12864-017-4190-8

Grimes, William. (2015). Jack Yufe, a Jew whose twin was a Nazi, dies at 82. *New York Times* (November 13). https://www.nytimes.com/2015/11/14/us/jack-yufe-a-jew-whose-twin-was-a-nazi-dies-at-82.html

Hämäläinen, Pekka. (2019). *Lakota America: A new history of indigenous power.* Yale University Press.

Hanyu-Deutmeyer, A. A., Cascella, M., and Varacallo, M. (2023). Phantom limb pain. National Library of Medicine. https://www.ncbi.nlm.nih.gov/books/NBK448188

Harrington, Anne. (2016). Mother love and mental illness: An emotional history. *Osiris, 31*(1): 94–115. https://doi.org/10.1086/687559

Hayasaki, Erika. (2018). Identical twins hint at how environments change gene expression. *Atlantic* (May 15).

Heard-Garris, N., Rhea Boyd, R., Kan, K., Perez-Cardona, L., Heard, N. J., and Johnson, T. J. (2021). Structuring poverty: How racism shapes child poverty and child and adolescent health. *Academic Pediatrics, 21*(8): S108–S116. https://doi.org/10.1016/j.acap.2021.05.026

Hilgard, Josephine R. (1953). Anniversary reactions in parents precipitated by children. *Psychiatry, 16*(1): 73–80. https://doi.org/10.1080/00332747.1953.11022910

His Holiness the 14th Dalai Lama of Tibet. (n.d.). "Reincarnation." https://www.dalailama.com/messages/retirement-and-reincarnation/reincarnation

Howle, E., and Cordiner, D. (2014). Sterilization of female inmates. *California State Auditor* (June 19). https://www.auditor.ca.gov/pdfs/reports/2013-120.pdf

Hughes, Virginia. (2014). Epigenetics: The sins of the father. *Nature, 507* (March): 22–24. https://www.nature.com/news/epigenetics-the-sins-of-the-father-1.14816

Jahan, Sharmin, Araf, Kazi, Griffiths, Mark D., Gozal, David, and Mamun, Mohammed A. (2020). Depression and suicidal behaviors among Bangladeshi mothers of children with Autism Spectrum Disorder: A comparative study. *Asian Journal of Psychiatry, 51* (June). https://doi.org/10.1016/j.ajp.2020.101994

Johns Hopkins Medical Institutions. (2008). Our genome changes over lifetime, and may explain many "late-onset" diseases. *ScienceDaily* (June 25). www.sciencedaily.com/releases/2008/06/080624174849.htm

Joshi, R. S., Rigau, M., García-Prieto, C. A., Castro de Moura, M., Piñeyro, D., Moran, S., Davalos, V., Carrión, P., Ferrando-Bernal, M., Olalde, I., Lalueza-Fox, C., Navarro, A., Fernández-Tena, C., Aspandi, D., Sukno, F. M., Binefa, X., Valencia, A., and Esteller, M. (2022). Look-alike humans identified by facial recognition algorithms show genetic similarities. *Cell Reports, 40*(8): 111257. https://doi.org/10.1016/j.celrep.2022.111257

Kellermann, Natan Pf. (2013). Epigenetic transmission of Holocaust trauma: Can nightmares be inherited?. *Israel Journal of Psychiatry and Related Sciences, 50*(1): 33–39.

Keysers, C., and Gazzola, V. (2014). Hebbian learning and predictive mirror neurons for actions, sensations and emotions. *Philosophical Transactions of the Royal Society B, 369*(1644). https://doi.org/10.1098/rstb.2013.0175

King Abdullah University of Science and Technology. (2018). "The long and the short of DNA replication. *Phys.org* (June 4). https://phys.org/news/2018-06-short-dna-replication.html

Kirshenbaum, Greer. (2023). *The nurture revolution: Grow your baby's brain and transform their mental health through the art of nurtured parenting.* Balance.

Klengel, Torsten, and Binder, Elisabeth B. (2015). Epigenetics of stress-related psychiatric disorders and gene × environment interactions. *Neuron, 86*(6): 1343–1357. https://doi.org/10.1016/j.neuron.2015.05.036

Klosin, A., Casas, E., Hidalgo-Carcedo, C., Vavouri, T. and Lehner, B. (2017). Transgenerational transmission of environmental information in *C. elegans. Science, 356*(6335): 320–323. https://doi.org/10.1126/science.aah6412

Koren, Marina. (2018). How did astronaut DNA become "fake news"? (2016). *Atlantic* (March 16).

Landhuis, Esther. (2018). How dad's stresses get passed along to offspring. *Scientific American* (November 8). https://www.scientificamerican.com/article/how-dads-stresses-get-passed-along-to-offspring

Leadbeater, C. W. (1918). *Clairvoyance.* Theosophical Publishing House.

Li, J., & Zhang, Q. (2017). Insight into the molecular genetics of myopia. *Molecular Vision, 23*, 1048–1080.

Linden, David. (2020). *Unique: The New Science of Human Individuality.* Basic Books.

Littlechild, Chris. (2018). The uncanny case of the Jim twins, two estranged twins who led identical lives. *Ripley's* (May 28). https://www.ripleys.com/stories/jim-twins

Loftus, E. F., and Palmer, J. C. (1974). Reconstruction of automobile destruction: An example of the interaction between language and memory. *Journal of Verbal Learning and Verbal Behavior, 13*(5): 585–589. https://doi.org/10.1016/S0022-5371(74)80011-3

Maas, R.P.P.W.M., and Voets, P.J.G.M. (2014). The vampire in medical perspective: myth or malady?. *QJM: An International Journal of Medicine, 107*(11): 945–946, https://doi.org/10.1093/qjmed/hcu159

Mackenzie, R. (2023). A mother's body retains cells from her child after pregnancy. *Technology Networks* (September 21). https://www.technologynetworks.com/immunology/news/a-mothers-body-retains-cells-from-her-child-after-pregnancy-379082

Mariani, M. (2015). The tragic, forgotten history of zombies. *Atlantic* (October 28). https://www.theatlantic.com/entertainment/archive/2015/10/how-america-erased-the-tragic-history-of-the-zombie/412264

McCrae, M. (2021). Birds have a mysterious "quantum sense." For the first time, scientists saw it in action. *ScienceAlert* (January 8). https://www.sciencealert.com/birds-have-a-quantum-sense-and-for-the-first-time-scientists-see-it-in-action

McFarling, Usha Lee, and STAT. (2018). Memory transferred between snails, challenging standard theory of how the brain remembers. *Scientific American* (May 14). https://www.scientificamerican.com/article/memory-transferred-between-snails-challenging-standard-theory-of-how-the-brain-remembers

Menakem, Resmaa. (2017). *My grandmother's hands*. Central Recovery Press.

Merheb, M., Matar, R., Hodeify, R., Siddiqui, S. S., Vazhappilly, C. G., Marton, J., Azharuddin, S., and al Zouabi, H. (2019). Mitochondrial DNA, a powerful tool to decipher ancient human civilization from domestication to music, and to uncover historical murder cases. *Cells*, 8(5): 433. https://doi.org/10.3390/cells8050433

Morgan, I. G., and Rose, K. A. (2019). Myopia: Is the nature–nurture debate finally over?. *Clinical and Experimental Optometry*, 102: 3–17. https://doi.org/10.1111/cxo.12845

Müller, F. Max. (Ed.). (1882). *The* Bhagavadgîtâ *with the* Sanatsugâtîya *and the* Anugîtâ. Trans. Kâshinâth Trimbak Telang. In *The Sacred Books of the East*, vol. 8. Clarendon Press. https://www.rarebooksocietyofindia.org/book_archive/196174216674_10154419998761675.pdf

National Institutes of Health [NIH], National Human Genome Research Institute. (2022). *Eugenics and scientific racism*. Fact sheet, updated May 18. https://www.genome.gov/about-genomics/fact-sheets/Eugenics-and-Scientific-Racism

NPR. (2019). What twins can tell us about who we are. Interview by Shankar Vedantam. *Hidden Brain* (March 25). https://www.npr.org/transcripts/705487258

Pained by a buried hand. (1888). *Columbus Enquirer-Sun* (December 17), p. 1. https://gahistoricnewspapers.galileo.usg.edu/lccn/sn84024799/1888-12-17/ed-1/seq-1

Paul, Annie Murphy. (2010). *Origins: How the nine months before birth shape the rest of our lives.* Hay House.

Popkin, G. (2018). Einstein's "spooky action at a distance" spotted in objects almost big enough to see. *Science* (April 25). https://www.sciencemag.org/news/2018/04/einstein-s-spooky-action-distance-spotted-objects-almost-big-enough-see

Riedinger, R., Wallucks, A., Marinković, I., Löschnauer, C., Aspelmeyer, M., Hong, S., and Gröblacher, S. (2018). Remote quantum entanglement between two micromechanical oscillators. *Nature, 556:* 473–477. https://doi.org/10.1038/s41586-018-0036-z

Rodgers, A. B., Morgan, C. P., Bronson, S. L., Revello, S., and Bale, T. L. (2013). Paternal stress exposure alters sperm microRNA content and reprograms offspring HPA stress axis regulation. *Journal of Neuroscience, 33*(21). https://www.jneurosci.org/content/33/21/9003.long

Rombes, Nicholas. (2014). *The absolution of Roberto Acestes Laing.* Two Dollar Radio.

Salvatore, J. E., Larsson Lönn, S., Sundquist, J., Sundquist, K., & Kendler, K. S. (2018). Genetics, the rearing environment, and the intergenerational transmission of divorce: A Swedish national adoption study. *Psychological Science, 29*(3), 370–378. https://doi.org/10.1177/0956797617734864

Schrempft, S., van Jaarsveld, C. H. M., Fisher, A., Herle, M., Smith, A. D., Fildes, A., & Llewellyn, C. H. (2018). Variation in the heritability of child body mass index by obesogenic home environment. *JAMA Pediatrics, 172*(12): 1153–1160. https://doi.org/10.1001/jamapediatrics.2018.1508

Schuster, Ruth. (2019). Worms help Israeli scientists rewrite basics of genetics. *Haaretz* (June 10). https://www.haaretz.com/science-and-health/worms-help-israeli-scientists-rewrite-basics-of-genetics-1.7345758

Segal, N. L., Montoya, Y. S., Loke, Y. J., & Craig, J. M. (2017). Identical twins doubly exchanged at birth: A case report of genetic and environmental influences on the adult epigenome. *Epigenomics, 9*(1): 5–12. https://doi.org/10.2217/epi-2016-0104

Severns, Maggie. (2012). Study offers possible explanation for the huge gender gap in science and math. *Slate* (June 14). https://slate.com/technology/2012/06/stem-gender-gap-research-on-telling-girls-they-re-bad-at-math.html

Shomrat, Tal, and Levin, Michael. (2013). An automated training paradigm reveals long-term memory in planarians and its persistence through head regeneration. *Journal of Experimental Biology, 216*(20): 3799–3810. https://doi.org/10.1242/jeb.087809

Shrivastava, S., Naik, R., Suryawanshi, H., and Gupta, N. (2019). Microchimerism: A new concept. *Journal of Oral and Maxillofacial Pathology, 23*(2): 311. https://doi.org/10.4103/jomfp.JOMFP_85_17

Thomas, Kara N., Srikanth, Nimisha, Bhadsavle, Sanat S., Thomas, Kelly R., Zimmel, Katherine N., Basel, Alison, Roach, Alexis N., Mehta, Nicole A., Bedi, Yudhishtar S., and Golding, Michael C. (2023). Preconception paternal ethanol exposures induce alcohol-related craniofacial growth deficiencies in fetal offspring. *Journal of Clinical Investigation, 133*(11): e167624. https://doi.org/10.1172/JCI167624

University of Minnesota. (2021). What happens when scientific findings conflict?. https://hsjmc.umn.edu/events/2021-05-18-what-happens-when-scientific-findings-conflict

Upadhyaya, S., Blocker, C. P., Rika Houston, H., and Sims, M. R. (2021). Evolving two-generation services to disrupt the intergenerational effects of poverty and promote family well-being. *Journal of Business Research, 125* (March): 324–335. https://doi.org/10.1016/j.jbusres.2020.12.019

Vinkers, C. H., Geuze, E., van Rooij, S. J. H., Kennis, M., Schür, R. R. Nispeling, D. M., Smith, A. K., Nievergelt, C. M., Uddin, M., Rutten, B. P. F., Vermetten, E., and Boks, M. P. (2021). Successful treatment of post-traumatic stress disorder reverses DNA methylation marks. *Molecular Psychiatry, 26*: 1264–1271. https://doi.org/10.1038/s41380-019-0549-3

Watson, Burton. (Trans.). (1971). *Records of the grand historian of China.* Columbia University Press.

Weinhold, Bob. (2006). Epigenetics: The science of change. *Environmental Health Perspectives, 114*(3): A160–167. https://www.ncbi.nlm.nih.gov/pmc/articles/PMC1392256

Weizmann Institute of Science. (1998). Quantum theory demonstrated: Observation affects reality. *ScienceDaily* (February 27). www.sciencedaily.com/releases/1998/02/980227055013.htm

Wilson, D. (n.d.). *African traditional religions textbook: Ifa.* Chapter 9: *The Holy Odus: 256 sacred parables, proverbs and prescriptions.* Robert W. Woodruff Library, Atlanta University Center. https://research.auctr.edu/Ifa/Chap9Intro

World Health Organization. (2022). *Schizophrenia.* https://www.who.int/news-room/fact-sheets/detail/schizophrenia

Zimmer, K. (2022). Do epigenetic changes influence evolution?

The Scientist (November). https://www.the-scientist.com/features/do-epigenetic-changes-influence-evolution-70591

Zuckerman, Catherine. 2019. One-of-a-kind study of astronaut twins hints at spaceflight's health effects. *National Geographic* (April 11). https://www.nationalgeographic.com/science/article/study-of-astronaut-twins-hints-at-spaceflight-health-effects

Acknowledgments

Writing this book has been a journey of vulnerability, courage, and connection—a journey I couldn't have undertaken alone. It is impossible to name everyone by name, but know that this book stands as a testament to the power of community—to the countless individuals who, through their support, wisdom, and encouragement, have helped shape its pages.

- First and foremost, I want to express my deepest gratitude to my husband and children, whose unwavering support and love sustain me through every challenge and triumph. And to Eric, whose patience and encouragement never wavered, thank you. I would have given up multiple times if it hadn't been for your persistence.
- To my incredible friends, whose dedication and brilliance in their own lives helped push me to bring my idea to life. And a special thanks to my female friends: your unwavering support, understanding, and laughter have been the pillars of strength throughout the journey of my life. In each of you, I have found inspiration, wisdom, and love. Thank you for the conversations filled with encouragement and insight, for the shared laughter that eased the burdens of the writing process, and for the countless moments of camaraderie that reminded

me of the power of female friendship. An extra special hug to the following:

- To Stephanie, Monika, and Laura, your endless enthusiasm and belief in my abilities have fueled my passion and kept me going even when doubt threatened to take hold.
- To my long-lost friend Sarah and to Cassie, your unparalleled wisdom and perspective have challenged me to think deeper, write clearer, and strive for excellence in every word.
- To Merb, Mary G, and Corinne your unwavering support and unwavering kindness have been a constant source of comfort and inspiration, reminding me that I am never alone on this journey.
- To Mary T., for meeting me in the darkness when no one else was there.
- And to each and every one of the women in my life who has lent an ear, offered a shoulder to lean on, or simply shared in the joy of creation—thank you all for being the sisters I never knew I needed.
- To Jeff, for being the best bookstore owner in the universe and a guide in this process. Thank you for being you and for your unwavering commitment to excellence.
- I am endlessly grateful to the courageous individuals who shared their stories, struggles, and triumphs with me. Your bravery inspires me more than words can express, and it is an honor to amplify your voices through these pages.
- To my mentor, Agnes Leshner, and to my colleagues and peer supervision group, thank you for your wisdom, guidance, and encouragement. Your insights have shaped my thinking and inspired me to push beyond my limits.
- To my editor, Todd Manza, who in addition to editing helped me immensely in finding the starting point for this whole crazy self-publishing madness.\

And to my readers—thank you for joining me on this journey. It is my deepest hope that the words within these pages bring you insight, inspiration, and empowerment.

With love and gratitude,
Crystal

Crystal Oakman, a dedicated mental wellness advisor, educator, and speaker, holds a Master's degree in Social Work. Her impactful work focuses on fostering empowerment, enhancing mental flexibility, and promoting emotional well-being. With a wealth of experience, Crystal has been recognized in esteemed publications such as The Chicago Tribune, BravoTV, NBC's Better, TeenVogue, and Bloomberg Businessweek. She also serves as a trusted mental health expert for WHAG and WDVM news, leveraging her expertise to provide valuable insights and support to the community.